SIMPLY

Radiant

SIMPLY

Radiant

Practical Wisdom to Turn Back the Years

Bharti Vyas

with Jane Warren

Thorsons

Thorsons
An Imprint of HarperCollins*Publishers*
77–85 Fulham Palace Road,
Hammersmith, London W6 8JB

The Thorsons website address is:
www.thorsons.com

Paperback edition first published by Thorsons 2001
10 9 8 7 6 5 4 3 2 1

© Bharti Vyas 2001

Bharti Vyas and Jane Warren assert the moral right
to be identified as the authors of this work

Text illustration by Paul Beebee

A catalogue record for this book
is available from the British Library

ISBN 0 7225 4035 3

Printed and bound in Great Britain by
Scotprint, Haddington

To my late mother Pushpaben Bhatt – my guiding spirit, and to my darling husband, Raja, my very much wanted daughters, Shailu and Priti, my beautiful grandchildren – Anjali, Neha, Saajan and Serena, and my two sons-in-law, Bharath and Parag, who are the closest thing to sons that I have.

Contents

Acknowledgments

To Jane Warren, who was an absolute pleasure to work with; Claire Haggard for my last book *Beauty Wisdom*; Dr Jeanette Ewin for giving me insight into nutritional health; Caroline Shott, Wanda Whiteley and Eileen Campbell for their continous support and guidance; Annie Lawton who was instrumental in introducing me to the medical world; my manageress Magda Reggio and all my staff at my centre; to Lorraine Kelly and Karen Hughes at GMTV, who have been so professional to work with and have given me the opportunity to share my knowledge on television; and the numerous journalists who have supported me throughout, these include Lisa Aziz, Janine Josman, Daisy Goodwin, Caroline Hogg, Lisa Podmore, Caroline Hendrie, Kate Sampson, Kathy Phillips, Sarwar and Samina Ahmed, Heather McGlone, Robina Dam and Michael Van Stratten; Janet Saunders who believed in me and took my products to the House of Fraser stores; to Cindy Martin and Melissa Fairhurst for continuing that support; to John Gustavon, Armand Beasley and Nikki Kinnaird; to Gail and Lindsay Booth and Dr Jean Ginsberg; my dear friends Jane Goldsmith and Hermie Hogg; and to Angela Westerhoff, Diane Maxwell and Peter Vaughan.

Author's note

I have chosen some strong and inspiring photographs for *Simply Radiant* of women actively enjoying their mid-life with confidence. I feel that many of us are tired of seeing a lack of positive images of mature, attractive women in the media. So here you have them – strong women in their prime, living life to the full!

Foreword

The human race is an integral part of this universe. So the essence of health is to live with nature. Human beings are designed to live in harmony with nature, but today we lead our lives more alienated from it than ever and often transgress its laws. Mechanization, fast food, our sedentary lifestyle and our polluted atmosphere have all affected our health and well-being. The stress and strain of modern life affects not only our body, but our mind and spirit too, for our emotional health is dependent to a surprising degree on our physical health.

The world has begun to recognize this fact and acknowledge the need for a more holistic approach to health than that provided by conventional Western medical thought. Bharti Vyas has produced a very timely testiment to the power of a holistic healthcare regime. She has integrated her vast experience and insight into health and beauty management in a simple and practical way. This book highlights the need for proper integration of all aspects of our mind, body and spirit for the preservation of health and beauty. This book takes a practical, down-to-earth approach to the different physical and psychological aspects of our changing bodies over our natural life span, and offers simple, natural measures to ease us through these changes. It offers important advice on the role of a healthy, balanced diet, with delicious and simple recipes. One of Bharti's most important insights for older women is her emphasis on the importance of a positive attitude.

As Ayurvedic practitioners, we found it especially interesting that many of the concepts described in this book concur with those of Ayurveda. Perhaps Bharti's Indian heritage gives her special insight. We feel it proves that Ayurvedic concepts, developed hundreds of years ago, are still relevant, even in this day and age.

We are sure that with her deep insight, knowledge and experience of the various physical, psychological and social factors of human life, Bharti and her magic hands will do much more useful work. We can expect more valuable contributions to come that will benefit all those concerned with health management

Dr G Vinod Kumar   Dr P K Lathika, BAMS
Medical Superintendant   Senior Physician
Kerala Ayurveda Pharmacy Ltd   Amrutham Ayurveda Hospital
Kerala, India   Kerala, India

Introduction

There is no magic formula for staying

You may be feeling that you can't tap into your energy as effectively as you would like to and be seeking advice on how to reinvigorate yourself. You may be concerned that your body is visibly deteriorating, and be casting around for a way to curtail the speed of these physical changes. If so, then you've bought the right book.

After the success of my first book, *Beauty Wisdom*, which I wrote to enable people to manage their own beauty care, without spending a fortune on expensive potions and lotions, I wanted to write a follow-up especially for the older woman, who may be feeling as though her body is being taken over by changes she can't understand or anticipate. It is my intention to explain the changes that your body may be going through and show what can be done, with a little determination and application, to retain and enhance your self esteem, embrace your increasing maturity and wisdom, and help slow down any physical deterioration in an holistic and entirely natural manner.

There is no magic formula for staying young and healthy forever, but there is a lot you can do to retain your vitality and youth well past menopause. If you are 35 plus, your body is changing chemically. But you

young, but there is a lot you can do

don't have to be swamped by these changes. The secret is to find a way to revitalize your inner self in the light of this metamorphosis. Western culture does not tend to prize age. But I will show you ways to embrace the benefits for yourself. When your spirits are high you will feel more attractive, happy and effective. As I always say to my clients: when you feel beautiful, you are beautiful. Beauty on the outside begins on the inside. Improved health and beauty can only be obtained by harmonizing mind, body and spirit. You really have to train yourself to feel beautiful. Confidence is more important than classical features, beautiful bones or the perfect figure.

You don't have to make radical, stressful changes. I am not trying to rewrite your lifestyle. It is best to view my advice as modifications you can introduce to enhance the life you *already* lead. To stay fabulous after 40 and 50, the little tweaks here and there can make a huge difference, for example, simply make sure you have enough calcium and walk a little further each day — if you exercise moderately for 30 minutes at least five times a week, you will almost halve your risk of a heart attack. And remember that everyday activities, such as DIY, walking and gardening, can be just as effective as swimming and cycling. Try to eat a little less: with every five years that pass after the age of 27 we need 50 calories a day less. Eat little and often during the day to maintain an even blood sugar level. And eat more in the mornings when your metabolic rate is at its highest and you are less likely to convert calories into fat. Drink at least two litres of water a day, avoid caffeine, but allow yourself a glass of red wine, which has positive benefits for your blood. Keep eating some fats, such as oily fish, olive oil and nuts, as they are essential for health. It's also a good idea to eat around 300g ($10^{1}/_{2}$oz) of fish each week, especially delicious oily fish such as tuna, mackerel, sardines, herrings and salmon.

The most important thing you can do about reaching mid-life is to feel high about it. This is my core philosophy. Today you know who you are and where you are going, so now is the time to embrace every second. Don't spend time thinking 'Oh I wish I had done that'. Do it now! Your thinking time is over. This is your doing time. Begin to make changes to any aspect of your life that makes you unhappy. And once you identify your concerns, don't waste another moment. What you can do today don't leave until tomorrow. If you can't make time to start then don't waste time worrying about it – you're expending unnecessary energy unless you can actually make a change.

Take personal responsibility for building yourself up and invest action into your life. Your mind and body are yours, and yours alone. You have total control of your purity: purity does not mean becoming a nun, it means doing whatever it takes to really like yourself.

Once you incorporate this positive philosophy into your life you will be surprised by how much pleasure you can gain from middle age. You have wisdom, focus and stability. You have an awareness of what you can and cannot achieve. Before you were 35 you were a generalist, now you have become a specialist. Whether your focal point is your household, friendships, creativity, work or relationship, now is the time to invest your power in it.

How you allow yourself to feel as you mature is largely your own choice. You are experiencing changes in your body, but that has no bearing on your ability to relish life. Realize the importance of investing time to nourish your confidence, sparkle, health, energy, vitality and looks as you age, and take good care of your skin, hair and clothes. All these things are connected to self esteem, the power source from which flows success in every other area of your life: work, children, your closest relationships. Learn to appreciate the body that you have. Don't try to focus a lot of time and effort on the things you can't change, but look openly at yourself and make a list of your best qualities.

The moment you start looking after yourself you will find that your whole attitude changes. If you decide to change your posture, to sit in a more upright way and to walk with more elegance you will increase your self esteem. Reward yourself with interesting food; make a rule that you won't eat the same meal twice in a week. If you find yourself thinking, 'Oh I can't go out today because I haven't done my hair,' ask yourself why you are limiting yourself. If you've worn your hair a certain way all your life – perhaps having it set or coping with lots of length – then go and have it cut. It can be invigorating to make a change. People will accept you as you present yourself. If you feel confident you will exude confidence and influence other people with your positive mood. Happiness is infectious, so seek out happy people with whom to spend your time. When you are happy you can't help but spread it around, however old you are.

Live your life as if you are going to live until you are 90. Work now to establish the behaviour that you would like to carry with you for the next 30, 40, 50 or 60 years. Your forties, fifties and sixties can be immensely invigorating if you can get the right thinking strategies in place now. You might be working less or beginning a new career. You may still be involved in raising your own children, or you might have become a grandparent and have the joy of being involved with young people without having to assume so much responsibility. Whatever situation you are in, look for the benefits that your wisdom and maturity can bring. Female film stars in their forties, fifties and sixties are in greater demand than ever: there's never been a better time to be middle-aged.

Embrace simplicity. Simplicity really boosts your energies. Men and women tend to spend their younger lives in a process of acquisitiveness: accumulating possessions and wealth. Now is the time to appreciate simple pleasures. Streamline your life. Make sure your house is a peaceful haven, somewhere you can go to relax and recharge your batteries. Yes, you want it to be clean, but don't keep it so clean that you feel uncomfortable

You have control over your own body:

living in it. Stop trying to impress people: this is a source of perpetual stress. Live by your own rule book. Quieten the chattering mind, let go of things that bother you, and don't hang on to negativity issued by other people. Don't worry about other people's unwarranted criticism: what you know doesn't fit, shrug off. Once you embrace this viewpoint, nothing unnecessary will get you down. If you get a few pimples, don't spend time agonizing that everyone you meet is worrying about them. Who's got time to look at your spots? Be honest enough to sort them out for you, and you alone.

I think the most tedious thing in the world is wondering how many carrots you're allowed for lunch. You have control over your own body, and being happy with yourself is the key. If you've got cellulite and you can live with it, then go ahead. But if you want to get rid of it, I don't go along with the line that wanting to enhance your attractiveness is wrong. As you age, you need less sleep. Embrace this as a boon. It leaves you with more hours in the day to get the most out of your life.

But where are you now? It is tempting, with the changes one's body undergoes before, during and after menopause, to feel eroded. For most women, menopause starts between the ages of 45 and 55, when the production of oestrogen by the ovaries starts to dwindle and decline. The resulting hormonal imbalances can lead to symptoms such as hot sweats, anxiety, irritability and poor concentration. At worst, some women suffer symptoms for between two and five years – but there are a wide variety of ways to minimize the impact of these problems, and although these changes can dent self esteem, for many women menopause is a welcome time of life, signalling the end of the dreaded monthly cycle.

Remember, however unnerving it may be, your body is showing the signs of age in an identical sequence to millions of other women.

being happy with yourself is the key

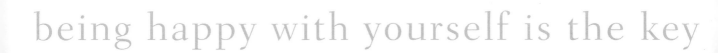

The first hint you received that you were beginning to get older was when you noticed that close-up in the mirror the skin on your face was no longer perfectly smooth. Fine lines were appearing around your eyes and mouth. Your jawline no longer seemed perfectly angular. Next, you became aware that the skin on your neck was losing some of its tone. You may have noticed a few white strands of hair appearing and become aware that your upper arms were filling out. Your thighs may have lost some of their firmness and the skin texture seemed less taut. Your stomach was more inclined to bulge and your bottom appeared to be acting increasingly under the influence of gravity.

Then one day you felt, or will feel, stiffening in your joints – this heralds increasing age finally creeping up on you from within your skin. This can be most disturbing, signalling a temptation to enter a decline and even begin to dress like an older woman. But in this day and age this is no longer necessary.

Unfortunately, for most of us, our physical prime arrives relatively early in our lives – around the age of 20. So what hope is there for 21-year-olds, let alone 40 or 50 somethings? Take heart: every age has its own kind of beauty – different elements of our looks flower and fade at different times. The secret is knowing how to enhance each passing perfection. While we may mourn the loss of taut skin and slender figures, we can look forward to clearer skin and glossier hair. We shouldn't dread the appearance of wrinkles, as a few laughter lines add character to your face.

The good news is that scientists claim that we are maturing better and living longer. But do educate yourself and safe-guard your health. Heart attacks are the biggest killer of post-menopausal women, and after menopause the risk of heart disease quadruples, so cut out greasy fry-ups and keep exercising. Nowadays, women are tenaciously holding on to their youth, and approaching milestones such as marriage and pregnancy later in life. Many women now feel confident delaying their families until their careers are established. The number of children born to mothers over 35 is now almost ten per cent of the total of births each year. At the same time, younger mothers may be watching their children leave home. So-called 'empty nest syndrome' can be very difficult to adjust to. Women who for so long have defined themselves in terms of their role as wife and mother, perhaps giving up or never embarking upon a career in the process, can feel dislocated and uncertain about what to do next. They can turn around and realize that there is little connecting them to their husband, who has often been busy ambitiously pursuing a career. This is a time of potential major crisis, and it is important that a woman learns to put herself first. Pamper yourself, sign up for some classes in a subject that interests you: be reflective by all means, but look for new activities to provide you with a sense of purpose and inner strength.

Having grandchildren can be one of the greatest pleasures in life, but it also takes a certain amount of readjustment to view yourself as 'the older generation', particularly if you still view yourself as a vibrant woman in her late prime. Embrace your changing role, relish the freedom your perspective gives you to love your grandchildren while enjoying the diminished responsibility that you have. Above all, kill any sort of thinking that makes you feel you have to behave like an old woman. The label 'grandmother' means your child has a child: it does not mean that you cannot enjoy sex, wear the latest makeup colours, or experiment with fashion — what it does mean is that you have more time to do so.

Although genes play an active role in an individual's propensity to age, the influences of lifestyle and behaviour are undeniable. Youth can be extended with a healthy diet, sensible exercise and a positive attitude. The message is clear: you are as young or old as you let yourself feel.

A QUICK GUIDE TO YOUR CHANGING BODY

TWENTIES

Face: Between the ages of 18 and 24 the contours of your face reached maturity. Skin is still too elastic for gravity to pull features down, but oily outbreaks are a problem.

Body: By the age of 25 your muscle strength, lung capacity and kidney function are at their peaks. Breast tissue is fully developed, but not filled out by additional fat.

Mind: The peak of ability to develop new skills and absorb information.

THIRTIES

Face: Gravity begins to pull your features downwards, but your cheek-bones become more defined and will remain so from now on. The clarity of your skin is in its prime, so experiment with makeup.

Body: To prevent the onset of osteoporosis in your mid-thirties you should start maintaining a high level of calcium. Don't crash diet as this causes sagging. Your breasts fill out to their full potential in size and shape, but need more support, so choose a kinder bra. Skin starts drying out in the mid-thirties as sebaceous glands slow down. Nails may start to peel and ridge, so keep skin moist with warm baths and moisturize all over.

Mind: With your ability to evaluate information in the light of experi-ence, your powers are crystal clear. Put your wealth of knowledge into action and be decisive. Sexual responsiveness peaks in your thirties, but a woman never stops enjoying sex.

Face: Wafer-thin skin around the eyes is the first to show signs of age, but gains extra translucence which should be highlighted by using brown tones on the cheeks and eye sockets. Lips shrink with age, but smile lines give added character.

Body: Muscle-tone needs more work now, especially buttocks and stomach, but as children leave home there is more opportunity to stick to an exercise program. Breast tissue begins to settle, but can stay pert if you swim.

Mind: Contrary to popular opinion, most mental capacities increase with age, and worldly wisdom can fill in any gaps.

I am always surprised by those who claim that when we reach menopause we have less energy. I don't believe this to be true. Yes, you are going through a change, but if you haven't actually got any diseased organs or medical problems then you will be alright. We tend to be overprotective about women who are going through menopause. Where is the rule book that says you suddenly become a redundant, infertile woman without purpose or physical vibrancy? The challenge is how to avoid such negative thinking. Instead, look for a whole new positive energy that will sustain you throughout mid-life. Use your menopause to your advantage. Try not to slow down too much. If you let it, your body will relax and then start going down hill. Don't look to menopause for excuses. We make our own luck, so create your own reality. Just because you have reached mid-life doesn't mean you should stop taking gambles. My life consists of taking gambles constantly and it gives me more energy than many young people.

Try not to think of menopause – a healthy stage of female maturity – as a disease to be treated. It is a natural transition to be experienced and, like puberty, will come to an end when, one magical day, your weight and moods will stabilize and your thinking will once again be informed by clarity. You made it through puberty *without* the benefits of wisdom and maturity: now that you have them, make sure you harness them to guide you.

If you are feeling a bit redundant, the best way you can become more effective is by discovering and harnessing your self esteem. Invest in yourself. There is a tendency for women to invest in everyone but themselves. Sexual confidence flows directly from self esteem, not from your looks, or age, or other people's judgements. In later years many women report that sex takes on a fresh new glow. There are a number of invigorating benefits

THIRTIES

CLAIRE, A STAINED GLASS ARTIST, 29

It was a bit of a shock when I looked in the mirror about a year ago and noticed fine lines creeping around my eyes. Although I've never been particularly worried about getting older, I did tend to think it was something that happens to other people. Then, a few months ago, I found a single white hair near my ear. I could no longer deny it: my thirtieth birthday was just a few months away. It was time to address the issues, update my image and give my body an MOT.

Firstly I arranged a smear test, which was a bit overdue and had been nagging at me. Thankfully I got the all clear. I also decided to stop taking the Pill, as I'd been on it for 12 years. Instead I had an IUD fitted, which is a more natural form of contraception, directly targeting the relevant area of my body, and means I can get on with my life without taking a daily pill.

I also decided to do something about my diet. Fortunately this to mid-life sex. If you have been together with your partner for a long time, you have a deep awareness of both your bodies; you might be working less and have more time to devote to matters of an intimate nature than when your house was full of children, and you still have the satisfaction of the connection and harmony between you. If you are in a new relationship, sex in the middle years is less likely to carry the risk of pregnancy and you are less likely to be as emotionally vulnerable as when you were younger. You have a certain security in yourself and a knowledge of what you do and don't expect from a loving relationship. You are happier to speak out about your likes and dislikes, and have evolved greater sexual knowledge.

coincided with a new relationship with a man who loves to cook. Rather than surviving on packet pasta, as I had before, we started ordering a weekly delivery of organic vegetables. Living in the middle of London, it is wonderful to have muddy vegetables in the fridge.

I've always worn my hair long, and although I'd had my girlish lengths shaped a bit last year, I decided it was time to go for a more sophisticated feathered look. Far from finding that my confidence was connected to my long, unstructured locks, I've had a lot more feedback with a style that is mid-length, much fuller and easier to look after. I've never been one for lotions and potions, and I'm allergic to women's magazines, but I'd heard about the benefits of fruit acids and AHAs. I've always suffered from dry, somewhat pimply skin, and my beauty routine extended no further than washing morning and evening with a gentle foaming cleanser. Now, my fiancé and I decided to invest in a day cream and a night cream which promise to help slow down the onset of more of those fine lines. Our skin already looks much smoother and it's nice to share the motivation of a dual beauty mission.

The mental advantages of age are powerful. As a young woman between the ages of 15 and 25 you have little hindsight to inform your life choices and daily decisions. In Gujarati we have an unflattering term we apply at this age: 'gadhapachisi', which means your brain is 'as thick as a donkey'. But after 25 the mind evolves and you can draw increasingly upon insight and perspective. By 35 your wisdom is at its sharpest. Once you embrace this sort of attitude, life becomes very enjoyable. You become aware of your own weaknesses and you have the tools to counter them effectively. It's human psychology to reach 35 and gloomily label yourself

FORTIES

SERENA, 43, AN ANALYST

With three active children and a full-time job as an economics analyst, it can be difficult carving out time to spend on myself. But I'm aware that any time I spend on my health and beauty routine ultimately benefits my family. If I'm able to stay fit, healthy and happy I'll be much more effective in every way.

In my late thirties I noticed that I was tending towards that dreaded English pear shape. I'm very sedentary in my job, so I decided to join a gym. After work, three times a week, I spend an hour on a step machine. Fortunately my mother lives nearby and is able to look after the children while I'm there when the nanny has gone home. She loves having a bit of concentrated time with them, and I come home glowing from my exertions. Better still, although I'm not obsessive, my shape has stabilized and although I've gone up a size in the past six years, my face is not looking at all wrinkled – it's a trade-off I'm happy to make.

old. But far from viewing encroaching middle age as a negative, adapt your thinking: now you have power to harness, and if you are focused it is possible to become even more successful from this point on. You have more skills and more ability to use them than at any point during your twenties.

The physical changes occurring in your body can trigger psychological and emotional reactions, but do not assume your looks will fade just because you have reached menopause. By taking good care of yourself you can continue to feel lively, youthful and sexually attractive. Increasing numbers of women are using hormone treatment, and its effects can be

I started getting quite a lot of grey hairs and realized I had two options: to do something or not. Rather than anything drastic, I now use a wash-in tint colour and it's definitely helped my confidence. I've also updated my wardrobe with some vibrant colours and if I'm feeling a bit down, I'll sling on something uplifting.

I've been feeling a bit irritable lately. I've always had a few days of lowered mood before my period, but recently I've had some brittle days every month or two that don't seem to be connected to anything that's going on around me. I spoke to my doctor and he suggested that this might be the beginnings of menopause. This was a bit of a surprise, as my youngest child is only two, and I'd always thought of being a grandmother when I go through the change. He offered me HRT, but I've decided to wait and see how things develop. Instead, I've bought some evening primrose oil capsules and I'm going to have a test for osteoporosis, which will ultimately be a deciding factor.

As a family we eat healthily, and I think this is really important. I try and buy foods that have not been genetically modified, and we eat raisins and nuts for snacks, rather than lots of biscuits and cakes.

extremely beneficial, but it is not essential: there are a number of other methods that can help you retain your joie de vivre.

Watching your weight; cutting down on foods that present a high risk of heart disease; increasing your uptake of calcium to help prevent osteoporosis; avoiding cigarettes; exercising regularly and staying mentally active are some of the key ways you can naturally maintain and prolong your health and happiness. The baby-boom generation, who are now starting to approach menopause, are very suspicious of putting chemicals into their bodies long-term after their experiences with the Pill. This means there is a need for non-drug and nutritional ways of helping women through the change. One approach, backed up by research reported recently in the *British Medical Journal*, is to take plants that have natural oestrogens in them, such as soya, linseed, ginseng and rhubarb, together with supplements of calcium, essential fatty acids and fish oil. St John's

FIFTIES

ROSEMARY, 53

I've never lacked confidence and I'm sure this has made things easier for me as I get older. I haven't yet begun menopause, but I wouldn't use HRT unless my bones needed it. I'd like to take a more holistic view and avoid drugs if I can.

I had some problems recently with poor skin and decided to cut out all wheat and dairy products for six months. I've noticed that the problem is definitely clearing up. If you look dreadful, you feel dreadful, and life's not much fun.

I've been aware, as I've been growing older, of updating my hair and my posture. These issues make a lot more difference to internal wort, or hypericum, fits with this approach very well. Hormone Replacement Therapy isn't very good at dealing with any loss of libido, while hypericum seems to be very effective, with few side effects.

HRT is a controversial area, which I will discuss in depth later. My own philosophy is to consider it for medical reasons, or if all else fails, but avoid using it solely to try and stay young. It can be very beneficial for women worried about osteoporosis, as it replaces the hormones that maintained bone mass in earlier life and can prevent fractures of the wrist, spine and hip as a result of loss of bone mass, but you should be aware that it can lead to fluid retention and weight gain, and an increased risk of developing breast cancer. If you choose not to use it, eating calcium-rich foods and certain vegetables can be an effective substitute in warding off osteoporosis, as can foods rich in phytoestrogens. These plant forms of oestrogen and progesterone are available naturally in various foods. They

confidence and external demeanor. You do see people sagging a bit, and if they are round shouldered they look much more weary than someone with lashings of white hair, standing upright and marching along happily.

My weight has been a problem, and I've put on two stone in the past ten years without eating more. But I'm comfortable with the way I look and, more importantly, I'm healthy. My partner and I go walking at least three times a week and we play badminton once or twice a month. I've never been a particularly beautiful woman, and he says he likes the cuddly me, so I feel quite secure. I'd much rather keep a good attitude to the weight gain, rather than starting to define myself in terms of it and worrying myself into a wrinkled face that I don't need.

have some hormone-balancing properties, but not at the high levels found in HRT treatments. The best protective oestrogenic foods include tofu (soya bean curd), rye bread, French beans and green lentils.

Try not to become obsessed with your weight. Concentrate on your inner landscape first. I am not a slim woman, but I know that when I remove my clothes and hold myself confidently I definitely attract my husband. A woman wearing designer clothes means nothing to a man if she doesn't have an attractive personality. Ultimately what men seek in a

SIXTIES

SUSAN, 60, A RETIRED JOURNALIST

My menopause started quite late. I wasn't on HRT or anything of that kind and was quite optimistic about menopause. I certainly had no feelings of dread. But I changed my mind halfway through. I thought I was enjoying the feel of my heart fluttering, but there was quite a lot of perspiration and I really went off the idea. I didn't have an absolutely awful time, but used some HRT towards the end.

Changing my thinking proved to be quite useful for me. Rather than worrying about things, I decided to take the approach that I would deal with whatever life threw at me in the most positive way I could. I've always had problem skin, which was quite damaging to my confidence. I realized that my skin was refusing to grow up. I'd been using a lot of makeup to mask the problem and couldn't go outside without my disguise. But gradually I realized that I could actually afford to take less trouble. So what if your skin is less than perfect? Why let your life revolve around it?

Now I have a regular massage and a facial. I come out of the clinic woman is someone warm and sexy, not a designer stick-insect. So lose your obsession with weight. Who you are and what you have to say is so much more important.

One of my daughters has put on weight since having her children. Recently we were going to a family wedding and because she was worrying that she had nothing to wear we went to a local market in South London, bought some fabric, made an outfit for her, and she was the talk of the whole evening. She wasn't the thinnest woman there by a long way, but

and get on the bus in public without a slick of lipstick. I've had lunch in restaurants on my own. I've walked down the street and had some of the nicest chats with taxi drivers in this denuded state. I've also had compliments.

I've learned finally to cleanse my skin with almond oil, which doesn't always come naturally to English women. It's amazing what you can do with your hands in terms of self massage. I put oil over my makeup and massage it off. I drink a lot more water now than I used to.

Since I've been having regular massage I have gained in confidence. I used to be embarrassed about taking my clothes off, but now I'll even wander around at home without a towel. This new openness has to some extent affected other areas of my life. I never used to discuss my skin with friends, and certainly not with total strangers, but recently I met a woman with a mark on her nose from cancer. She was distressed and self-conscious. I told her that I understood how she felt and that I'd always had to disguise my skin. She looked so relieved. I wouldn't have been able to do that before.

she held herself confidently and indulged in some fantastic Indian dancing. Yes, she's made a note to lose some weight, but she was able to put that ambition into perspective. She didn't let herself get depressed and wear something dull, or worse, not go at all. Instead, she shone. She is a wonderful lesson to any overweight woman. Enjoy today because time is not going to wait for you. Dress for comfort. Why strap yourself into designer clothes you don't enjoy, or diet obsessively and miss out on the sensuality of food? Better to be happy-go-lucky and wear something less expensive with a bit of panache. A carefree nature is much more healthy than striving for some impossible ideal.

Putting on a few pounds is not something we should become obsessed

SEVENTIES

PAMELA, 78

I was lucky that the women in my family have always looked young for their years, and that until his death five years ago, my husband was always very adoring of the way I looked. I do think that personality and internal confidence are much more important than external things, so I was lucky I had a husband who clearly agreed with me. And it's a good thing I wasn't too worried, because when you look in the mirror and see an old lady looking back it's actually rather a shocking thing. Sometimes I don't recognize myself when I see a little old lady with white hair reflected in shop windows. Inside I still feel about 21, as I always have. The greatest physical change I noticed was three summers ago. I've always had a summer and winter wardrobe, and in the summer would wear cotton dresses with short sleeves. When I got out the dresses and put one on, I couldn't believe that my upper arms about. Having some extra padding on your frame is not bad for you as long as it is not excessive. But if you find the extra weight is inhibiting or restricting your lifestyle, or if you find walking, breathing or moving difficult, you must heed the warning of your puffing, panting or aching. Your body is telling you to lose weight and you should listen to it.

As a holistic practitioner I always counsel my clients to listen to their bodies. I believe that many of the diseases we suffer are, to a certain extent, self-inflicted. I use the analogy of a tourist going on a tropical holiday to a country where malarial mosquitoes are common. Our tourist ignores the health guidelines, doesn't take anti-malarial tablets and contracts malaria. That is my definition of a self-inflicted illness.

were all wobbly and had grown in size. I'd never consider surgery: why interfere with something that is a perfectly natural part of getting older? Instead, I bought myself a nice lacy cardigan to wear over the top.

I've never believed in spending fortunes on the way you look. I used to have my hair set, which was my one indulgence, but now I've gone for a more modern, elfin, wash-and-go sort of style, which I really like. My skin has become quite wrinkled since I've been in my seventies, but for years and years people were amazed at how line-free I was. My secret? Olive oil applied each night before I go to sleep.

I try to keep my mind active by reading voraciously, which seems to me to be the most effective way of keeping the years at bay. And although I live in sheltered accommodation, I try to get out for regular walks in the nearby village. I've always eaten sensibly and don't buy processed foods. I eat fish once a week, a little lean red meat, and lots of fruit and vegetables. I feel as well as I possibly can, which is a wonderful thing to be able to say at nearly 80.

The same thing happens when your body gives you any sort of signal that some element of its functioning is under stress – a headache, a tummy ache, a skin condition. If you don't take any notice and continue to live at the same pace, eating the same body-congesting foods, sleeping minimally, smoking or drinking, you are doomed to exacerbate your symptoms. If you ache what is your body trying to tell you? Please rest me, or protect me from the sun, or feed me more sensibly. You have tired arms. What are they trying to tell you? You overwork me. Do we listen? No, we carry on and that is when more damage is done inside the body. Wear and tear become higher until you push your resources so far that you become depressed, you cannot sleep, you can't repair yourself and eventually you become ill.

The basis of holistic thinking is that all the different elements of the body and mind are fundamentally interconnected. Try to foster a belief in the self-diagnosis that we so often choose to ignore, or to cover over with a well-intentioned painkiller rather than making a change to some part of our life. Each cell in your body is able to replicate constantly for over 100 years, but we overburden our system rather than nourish it gently.

Until we are about 35 our energy works differently and we can afford to ignore a few signs and signals. But after 35 don't ignore any of them. Take them seriously and make sure you really look after yourself, both internally and externally. If you choose to ignore a warning your body is much more likely to give you a problem.

You can also use your body's own healing power in a quite simple, but potent, way. If you are feeling tired or you have a sore muscle, avoid taking a painkiller. Far better is to lightly rub the area with your hands for five to ten minutes. If your eyes are tired, perhaps through concentrating on a computer screen, place your palms upon your closed eyelids and push. After a few minutes your eyes will feel recharged.

Always remember that the change of life can bring positive

Each cell in your body is able to

transformations. Margaret Mead coined the term 'Menopausal Zest' to remind us that some mid-life women feel better than ever before. You too can enjoy an increased sex drive, creativity and energy, greater confidence, awareness of your body's needs, improved self esteem and enhanced communication skills.

One of the secrets of my success as a therapist is that people come to me and I say, 'Leave your problems with me, you go ahead and enjoy life.'

My intention is that this book will help you address some of the issues you face as you age, giving you the confidence to find effective solutions to the problems that crop up as you mature, while freeing you up to get on with the things that really matter.

BHARTI'S OWN STORY

I am now 56 and my career has really taken off over the past 15 years. The secret of my mid-life success? My mind was already mature. This meant I knew how to focus my abilities and apply myself to things. Through experience I also had faith in my own energy levels, which meant I knew what I was capable of and wasn't afraid to push myself.

I married my husband, Raja, in March 1964 and had my two daughters when I was 21 and 23. We moved to Britain in 1968, and I worked at an insurance company before buying a delicatessen and working 12 hour days for nine years. Raja was working full time at a bank and would help me at the shop after I had fed the children and picked him up from work. We had a will to succeed and within five years we had bought the lease of the entire building; ten years later we owned the freehold. When I bought the shop it was taking £150 a week, within six months we were taking £1500 a week. I was working very hard … whatever I take on, I put in 100 per cent of my ability: that way, if I fail I will know that it is through no fault of my own.

plicate constantly for over 100 years

At the age of 35 I had an ectopic pregnancy and nearly died. It forced me to make changes because I was very weak. Raja wanted me to take a year's rest, but I'm not one to sit at home. Instead I went on a beauty therapy course, thinking that I could pass on my knowledge to my family. My interest in therapy has always had a very pragmatic, holistic core.

Part of my training was work experience in a salon and a sign on the street would offer our student therapies at reduced prices. One of my clients was an American. After I'd finished her facial she rested her hands upon mine and said, 'Bharti, these hands are magic. Let me take you to Las Vegas and we'll open a beautiful salon for you to work with these tools.' I was flattered, but taken aback that her enthusiasm went so far as to want to invest in me. Overjoyed, I went home and told Raja. He is a very steady man, and he listened to me intensely. It wasn't until the next morning that he said, 'Bharti, it is wonderful that someone wants to invest in you, but if you wish to be a therapist why not work in London?' Of course he was right. We couldn't have disrupted our family life in such a way. I turned down my investor, but she had given me the seed of realization that I had some special ability resting in my hands.

A few months later the same client went for a treatment in a department store with which she was dissatisfied. The manager told her how difficult it was to get a good therapist, to which she replied, with typical American gusto, 'You want a good therapist? I'll tell you where to go.' And so it was that I ended up working in a leading department store beauty franchise as a consultant.

After nine months I resigned. I did not like the attitude of some of the people I came across, and by now I knew for certain I was a good therapist. It was then that I decided I was never again going to work for someone else. So, when I was 39, I set up a small beauty concession in a local hairdressing salon and was phenomenally busy. I invested wisely in equipment and learned acupuncture and laser treatment.

In 1982 I was approached by a leading West End hair salon and took over all their beauty concessions, which gave me four salons in the best parts of London, employing 20 staff.

All went well until I had a car accident in November 1986 while on business in Israel. My left foot was shattered and became gangrenous. Although I did not have to have an amputation, as was feared at one stage, walking was extremely painful. But it was when my older daughter became pregnant that I made up my mind that my grandchild would not have a grandmother who could not take her out. And that got me going. It was nine months before I was back on my feet.

However, I had a problem. My salons were all in basements, which were difficult for me to access. It was time to buy my own salon. This was a blessing in disguise. I now have two salons employing 20 staff and handling 940 treatments a week. My clients include many celebrities. I have recently launched my own range of beauty products, following a four-year development process.

I have not yet been through menopause. I started my period quite late, when I was 17, and had no problems conceiving my daughters. Symptoms of menopause have not affected me yet, although four years ago I was getting a lot of lower back pain. My doctor gave me a bone density check and discovered I was losing calcium in my lower back. He advised me to use HRT to control the leeching calcium, so for three years I used it. When I returned for a second bone density check it was confirmed that the problem had been corrected and there was no reason to stay on HRT. Now I would only use it if my bone density deteriorates again. My periods continue to be regular as clockwork, although for the past ten years they have been getting progressively lighter and last only four days. I am a fairly placid person, fortunately I'm not troubled by mood swings and I rarely get irritable. Partly this is because I have a calm way of dealing with life. Raja and I have a very healthy sex life.

Age has given me the wisdom to deal well with people and an ability to find the confidence to delegate. Delegation is not an easy job. You have to know well enough what it is you want to be able to communicate this effectively to someone else. An ability to diversify has also been vital to my success. Make no mistake, I'm not superwoman, but I have never limited myself to the expectation that I can do only one thing at a time. And because I love what I do, which is vital, I still have energy left over. Every woman in her prime can benefit from this thinking.

THE ELEMENTS OF

Getting Older

With wisdom and confidence one can

Menopause

Your menopause is the most significant symptom of advancing age that you will experience. You are moving from a time of fertility to a time of reflection. No longer are you defined in terms of your ability to bear children and nurture life; instead you are approaching your role in the older generation. For many women such fundamental changes are profoundly disturbing. For others, they are a blessed relief.

With the right mind-set and knowledge, I believe it is possible for every woman to actively embrace her mid-life and gather up the benefits that wisdom and confidence make available. But in order to achieve this happy state of inner confidence and outer radiance, you must first navigate a certain number of physical and psychological symptoms. The good news is, there is light on the other side. You will come through your menopause vital, strong, confident and dynamic if you follow my holistic advice for easing any problems and enhancing your mental attitude.

First, an explanation of what actually happens to you as you approach mid-life. Put simply, menopause happens when your ovaries run out of eggs and your levels of the female hormone, oestrogen, fall. This in turn

Did you know...

Zinc helps fight infection and aids the process of wound healing. Good sources include wholegrain cereals, egg yolk, dairy products and red meat.

Zinc works with vitamin C, so plan your meals to include fresh vegetables and fruits along with zinc-rich foods.

embrace mid-life and reap its benefits

means that the lining of your womb is no longer expelled every month and so your periods stop. Menopause typically starts around the age of 40 and it can take 10 years until it is actually finished and you have your final period. At this point you can no longer conceive and you no longer have to contend with a monthly bleed – two facts that delight the majority of women. At the point when you have your menopause, you typically have around 40 per cent of your life left, so there is a wonderful incentive to make up for the discomfort menopause causes three out of every four women: the rest of your life! The longer you live, the longer you can expect to live. A baby may have a life expectancy of 75 years, but a 75-year-old woman can expect to live for at least another 12 years. The average woman will live for another 25 to 30 years after her menopause – and some for much longer.

In order to give ourselves the best possible chance of maturing gracefully, it helps to understand how we can expect our bodies to alter now that our ovaries are no longer producing oestrogen. So many of the changes we notice in our appearance as we approach and go through our menopause are the result of less oestrogen. This decrease in natural hormone has unfortunate side effects: we are likely to put on weight, particularly around the middle; we have an increased tendency to spots and acne; we might notice the appearance of excess facial hair; development of cellulite and darker patches of pigmentation; thinning hair and even hair loss. Worrying about these changes is a natural reaction, but excessive concern can lead to stress, which in turn exacerbates the problems. Understanding which skincare routines, changes in diet, herbal remedies, homeopathic solutions and relaxation exercises can really help goes a long way towards limiting the influence of these changes.

STAGES OF MENOPAUSE

Broadly speaking, there are three stages to the menopause, each with particular symptoms.

Did you know...

Zinc and copper work together to strengthen the immune system and slow deterioration of your skin. Life-bearing foods (nuts, grains and pulses/legumes) are good sources of both mineral micronutrients.

STAGE ONE: PERI-MENOPAUSE

Three to ten years before your menopause you may experience hot sweats during your period, mood changes, irregular and more frequent bleeding. Your body is gearing up to the end of your periods. Although the most intense part of this transition occurs two to four years before your menopause, your body is laying the hormonal groundwork for far longer than that. Your premenstrual symptoms begin to become more severe, your body shape changes as your stomach thickens, and you put on weight.

STAGE TWO: MENOPAUSE

This is when your periods stop (unless they have already been stopped artificially by a hysterectomy). Your periods can become very erratic at this time and you will only know you have had your last bleed when you have not had one for a year. Your body is gearing up for the changes you will experience after your monthly cycle stops.

STAGE THREE: POST-MENOPAUSE

Once you have stopped having periods, your hormone balance begins to change and this affects your body in a number of discomfiting ways. 75 to 80 per cent of women experience some combination of hot sweats, palpitations, high blood pressure, weight gain, distension, vaginal dryness and thinning of the bones.

THE BENEFITS OF HRT

Did you know...

Research suggests cabbage
contains substances that
protect against ovarian and
breast cancer by increasing
the speed at which excess
oestrogen is destroyed by
the body.

Imagine a drug that keeps our bodies younger and firmer, makes our hair glossy, keeps our skin clear, our bones healthy, and increases our sex drive. Now imagine that you don't have to pay for it, or take it. Instead, for 35 to 45 years, you naturally make this chemical for yourself. Oestrogen is our beauty and health powerhouse, the sex hormone that defines us as women and helps so many of our systems to run smoothly.

Unfortunately, at the time of menopause, our supplies of this substance dry up. Our bodies are designed to stop making oestrogen, but unfortunately there are a number of physical changes that occur as a result of the removal of this hormone from our systems. These include hot sweats, difficulty sleeping, vaginal dryness, lowered sex drive, bladder problems, loss of skin sensitivity, irritability, mood swings, anxiety and tearfulness. Because of these withdrawal issues, some doctors view menopause as a hormone deficiency disease and effortlessly advocate artificial oestrogen, in the form of HRT.

Personally, I find this view rather extreme, because unfortunately there are some significant disadvantages to taking HRT. However much the plus points speak to you, I would really advise you to discuss your own needs with your doctor. It is possible to live a happy and fulfilled life after menopause using purely natural techniques, so unless you really need it I would tend to counsel against taking HRT purely for cosmetic reasons. For although HRT dramatically reduces the risk of heart disease, it has been shown to increase the risk of uterine cancer and there is also a slightly increased risk of breast cancer. Additionally, it can lead you to have a monthly bleed (even though you no longer release an egg) and create quite severe premenstrual tension. If you have had a hysterectomy, you cannot get uterine cancer and in that case HRT is usually acceptable for its positive effect on your heart, and the other internal and external

THE THREE TYPES OF HRT

At present there are three main types of HRT available.

- The first is the older form of HRT, which contains oestrogen alone. This was found to increase the risk of cancer of the womb lining as it was not being shed every month. This type of HRT is now given only to women who have had a hysterectomy.
- The second and most widely used form of HRT is that in which oestrogen alone is taken for the first half of the monthly cycle with the addition of progesterone in the second half, creating a monthly bleed similar to a period. This is the main disadvantage of this form of HRT for most women, but it doesn't increase the risk of cancer of the womb lining.
- Thirdly, there is a newer sort of HRT in which both the hormones are combined to prevent the need for a monthly bleed, while still protecting against the cancer.

comforts that it can offer. Other women strike a compromise and take HRT for six to 12 months to see them through the worst part of their menopause, and then stop once their symptoms reduce in intensity.

I will discuss the beauty benefits of HRT in some depth, but also offer some natural menopause-without-medicine alternatives for those women who cannot, or choose not to, take it.

HRT aims to prevent the symptoms of menopause by replacing the oestrogen and progesterone no longer produced by the ovaries. Before menopause, oestrogen prepares the lining of the womb for a pregnancy every month and stimulates the production of an egg. When you take HRT, you are exposing your body to the levels of hormone it would receive if your ovaries were still producing it. (This is quite different from the artificially high levels of hormone that oral contraceptives offer in order to fool the body into thinking it is pregnant, so the risks of HRT are certainly lower than the risks of the Pill.) When a pregnancy does not occur, the body produces another hormone, progesterone, which sheds the unwanted womb lining. Replacing lost oestrogen is believed to cut the risks of brittle bones by 70 per cent. For women at risk of osteoporosis, HRT is usually prescribed for the five to ten years following menopause.

Oestrogen – whether natural or artificial – has a number of positive benefits for your body. It improves the condition of your skin and hair: hair is glossier and skin is softer, more flexible and less inclined to spots or blackheads, as oestrogen thins down the natural oils our skin produces. It also increases the production of new bone, keeps your tissues elastic (in particular your skin and blood vessel walls), lowers your cholesterol levels and stops your arteries furring up, helps regulate your sex drive and helps to produce the lubrication needed for comfortable love-making.

Falling levels of oestrogen are directly responsible for some of the most unsettling and painful elements of menopause. The following are all symptoms of oestrogen withdrawal:

- hot sweats
- difficulty sleeping
- vaginal dryness
- bladder problems
- loss of skin sensitivity
- migraine.

Oestrogen improves and maintains th

There are also some other physical changes you may notice in your body. They occur partly as a normal result of getting older, but they are made worse by a lack of oestrogen. They include:

- thinning of the skin
- patches of discolouration
- an increase in acne
- thinning hair
- increased facial hair
- a spreading waistline
- tiredness and lack of energy.

HRT can be useful for women suffering from hot sweats, bladder problems, loss of concentration and vaginal dryness. It might also help women at high risk of heart disease, Alzheimer's or osteoporosis who also have a poor diet and stressful lifestyle. It is not normally recommended for anxiety, depression and fatigue. If you decide to use HRT, your doctor can prescribe it in pill, patch, implant or vaginal cream forms.

NATURAL ALTERNATIVES TO HRT

If you cannot or would prefer not to take HRT, but would like to mimic some of the benefits that oestrogen gives your body during menopause, there are alternative options. Natural herbs cannot completely replace the long-term benefits of HRT, but many plants do contain chemicals that can relieve some of the symptoms of menopause. Phytotherapy is the use of plant extracts for healing, and it's not mumbo-jumbo: early pioneers in phytotherapy discovered that the willow tree contained the chemical we now know as aspirin, and there are numerous other examples.

condition of your hair, nails and skin

PHYTOESTROGENS

Most excitingly, certain plants have recently been found to manufacture natural chemicals that mimic female hormones. The secret to naturally minimizing hot sweats, headaches and palpitations is to eat the food whose properties most closely mimic the effect of the body's natural hormones. They can be used as ingredients for anyone, but are particularly beneficial to menopausal women. Foods rich in phytoestrogens (or plant oestrogens) include:

- soya beans
- linseed oil
- green and yellow vegetables
- ginseng
- fennel
- broccoli
- rhubarb
- celery.

It is also possible to take plant oestrogens in the form of linseed tablets. Other foods with hormone-balancing properties are:

- sprouted seeds and grains (such as alfalfa)
- yam
- papaya
- bananas
- figs
- garlic
- raw, unpasteurized honey.

Of the medicinal herbs, hops and sage are especially rich in plant oestrogens.

But of all the options, it is soya that is something of a wonder phytoestrogen. It is so effective that it is actually extracted commercially to manufacture some types of synthetic hormone products. A diet rich in soya may protect against breast cancer if you start taking it before menopause. Research has shown that women in China and Japan who eat a soya-rich diet have a lower incidence of breast cancer and little experience of hot sweats. Work in the UK also shows that increasing the amount of soya in the diet of pre-menopausal women lengthens the menstrual cycle by two days. This is beneficial because it lessens the time that breast tissues are exposed to the higher levels of oestrogen produced just before a period begins. Cooking with natural soya products is a very healthy way to help your body. Use soya milk in place of cows' milk, and cook with tofu and tempeh in place of meat. You can also used miso – fermented soya bean paste – as a tasty stock for soup.

The dried root of the black cohosh plant is a herbal remedy that also contains oestrogen-like plant hormones, and it can help to overcome some of the menopause symptoms that are due to a lowering of oestrogen levels.

However, minor deficiencies of vitamins and minerals might also be contributing to your general malaise, so it's a good idea to top up your diet, however sensible already, with a good multinutrient supplement, particularly one that has a mix of B-group vitamins.

EVENING PRIMROSE OIL

This pale liquid is a whole pharmacopoeia in a capsule. It is a rich source of an essential fatty acid that is a vital building-block for hormones. Evening primrose can naturally help to sort out breast pain, menopausal symptoms and dry, itchy skin. It is made even more effective when taken with vitamin E capsules, which help the body to hold onto its reserves of evening primrose oil. The valuable oil of evening primrose seeds provides a rich source of gamma-linolenic acid – an essential fatty acid used to keep cells in the body healthy. This cannot be obtained by diet alone.

NATURAL PROGESTERONE

Natural progesterone cream is extracted from wild yams and can help prevent osteoporosis. Applied regularly onto a part of the body where the skin is thin, such as the inner arm, (but not the eye area) it is also a good way to enhance mood and general wellbeing.

ST JOHN'S WORT

An excellent alternative to HRT is the herbal remedy, St John's wort, extracted from the shrub that grows alongside roads and railway cuttings. Hypericum, as it is also known, is now the biggest selling anti-depressant in Germany, outselling Prozac. Trials show that it is just as effective and has fewer side effects. It is now available over the counter in this country. It can help boost low mood and was used historically to treat mild depression throughout Europe. It is particularly good at restoring lost interest in sex. After taking hypericum for four weeks, only five to ten per cent of women were still off sex, while up to 70 per cent had rediscovered the joys of regular sex and even began initiating it! It can lift mild depression within two weeks of starting a course, with optimum results achieved after six. It can also help rid you of anxiety, agitation, insomnia and even headaches.

A good homoeopathic suggestion for helping to treat low mood is pulsatilla 30C, which is effective if you can't stop crying; or nux vomica 30C if your low mood is connected to stress, irritability and overwork.

Did you know...

Smoking causes a flood of free radicals to form in your body. This hastens the onset of the visible signs of age. If you smoke: give it up. It you fail to do that, make sure your diet contain foods rich in antioxidants including vitamin C, vitamin E and beta-carotene. Life-bearing foods are rich in vitamin E. Green, red and orange fruits and vegetables contain vitamin C and beta-carotene.

PSYCHOLOGICAL SYMPTOMS OF MENOPAUSE

Many women enter menopause with very low expectations. They approach their mid-life years with a certain dread, fully believing they are about to become emotional wrecks. In fact, although this is true for some women, it is far from usual. However, when the menopause does create psychological symptoms they can be every bit as real and distressing as some of the physical symptoms.

Irritability is connected to falling oestrogen levels and is more likely to be experienced by women who suffered pre-menstrual syndrome. It can be caused by not getting enough sleep, one symptom of lowered oestrogen levels, but might also be due to low blood sugar levels. If you are feeling irritated drink a glass of freshly squeezed orange juice, followed by a crisp-bread, slice of brown bread or a banana. You should feel an instant lift.

Anxiety makes you feel dread and impending doom, and can lead to symptoms similar to those caused by stress such as dizziness, loose bowels, muscle tension, flushing, palpitations and restlessness. The good news is that when anxiety is caused by menopause it tends to get better by itself. It is made worse by drinking alcohol or coffee, so the kindest treatment you can give yourself is to cut these out. If you are experiencing chest pains and palpitations you might be over-breathing (hyperventilating). This is very uncomfortable and the best treatment is to place a paper bag over your nose and mouth and breathe in and out to calm yourself down.

You might also like to try the homoeopathic remedy calc carb 30C, especially if you are also experiencing panic attacks, or phosphorus 30C which is used to treat continual underlying anxiety.

Mood swings can leave you feeling out of control as you ride the emotional roller coaster from high to low. Some women who feel less emotionally stable are right to highlight falling oestrogen levels as a cause, but in other cases do look at your current situation. If you are caring for an elderly relative, coping with an empty nest after your children have left home, or dealing with your changing self image, perhaps as you become a grandparent for the first time, your moods may be perfectly understandable symptoms of a stressful and changing environment.

The best thing you can do is take regular energetic exercise. Even going for a brisk walk on a daily basis can help you keep your mood swings under control. Exercise releases brain chemicals called endorphins that lift mood. Aim for exercise that leaves you slightly out of breath and increases your heart rate to around 110 beats a minute. HRT also has benefits here, if you can take it, and St John's wort has distinct benefits (cross ref to natural alternatives to HRT).

However, if you are feeling increasingly tearful, and feel your mood swings are getting out of hand, you might be suffering from a mild clinical depression. A certain amount of tearfulness is to be expected at menopause because of falling oestrogen levels, but watch to see your mood does not fall so low that you feel a sense of despair on waking. Depression is caused when certain brain chemicals become unbalanced. But because changing hormonal levels are the most common trigger in menopausal women, a doctor is most likely to recommend a course of HRT. If you are in any doubt as to the severity of your mood disorder, do go and see your doctor who can provide qualified advice.

STRESS

One area to try to control is the amount of stress in your life. Stress isn't just unsettling, it actually has a profound effect upon your experience of menopause. If you are under more pressure than you can comfortably handle, you are more likely to suffer menopausal symptoms. This is because you have exhausted your adrenal glands. Your adrenal glands make adrenaline – the heart-thumping, extra chemical boost you feel in moments of high tension or fear that enables you to react fast should you need to – but they also have a secondary role in menopause. When your ovaries cease to manufacture oestrogen, extra oestrogen is produced by the adrenal glands, but if they've been working flat out due to your high-stress lifestyle they have no extra reserves and you will be left feeling a mix of stress symptoms coupled with menopausal symptoms.

The best way to sort yourself out, second to reducing the stress in your life, is using a breathing exercise. If you breathe with quick, shallow breaths you are sending messages to your brain that you are under stress and the adrenal gland will continue to pump out its 'fight or flight' chemical. Actively controlling the way you breathe can trick your brain into thinking you are less stressed than you are and because you then produce less adrenaline, you really do become less stressed.

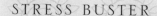

STRESS BUSTER

Use this exercise whenever you feel stressed. It takes only two minutes and no-one will notice.

- Sit back in your chair.
- Hang your arms by your sides, pulling your shoulders down and back.
- Take a deep breath, expanding your chest and filling your lungs to capacity.
- Breathe in and out very deeply, concentrating on the rise and fall of your abdomen.
- Do this five times, then breathe normally, counting to three as you inhale and four as you exhale.

Exercise is a brilliant stress reliever. Adrenaline primes you for activity; by exercising you will burn it up and afterwards find your stress levels have been reset to a more comfortable level. Caffeine and nicotine are a really bad idea if you are stressed, as they mimic the effects of adrenaline. You also need to keep your blood sugar levels fairly constant if you are stressed, so eat little and often, and don't miss meals. Try to eat at least five servings of fresh fruit and vegetables every day, and cut back on processed food, sugar, salt and saturated fats. A good herbal remedy for anxiety and nervous tension around menopause is motherwort. The leaves have been used for over a thousand years to regulate a fast pulse and lower blood pressure.

PHYSICAL SYMPTOMS OF MENOPAUSE

DEALING WITH HOT SWEATS

Most women experience hot sweats at some time. During the peri-menopause they can occur during your period, but once your periods have stopped you may be plagued for up to two years with these unsettling episodes that can last between one and five minutes. They are caused when chemicals are released that make the blood vessels dilate, blood rushes to the skin and your pulse may increase, creating palpitations. After the first flush passes through, your body then compensates for the extra heat that has been created by sweating. Your blood pressure may also drop for a moment, creating a sensation of dizziness.

Although harmless, the sudden sensation of heat that consumes face, neck and chest, sometimes followed by clamminess and sweating, can be upsetting and annoying. But remember, you probably feel hotter than you appear and sometimes you may not even flush pink at all.

The simplest way of minimizing your sweats is to avoid stimulants such as tea, coffee and alcohol. Cut out heat-giving food like garlic, onions and spices and remember that stress and tension also make sweats worse. Wear several layers of lighter clothing so you can adapt to different temperatures and consider not wearing a bra, as you may feel more comfortable without one.

Eat plenty of fruits, such as pears and apples, which calm down the system, and drink plenty of cold water. Try not to view water as a horrible medicine, flavour it with a dash of apple juice or buy aniseed water with rock sugar, which is a drink often given in temples located in hot parts of India – it will calm your system down while re-energizing you.

I am a great believer in a cold shower: it works wonders. You should avoid hot baths. If you are really troubled by the number or degree of hot sweats you are experiencing, consider taking HRT, which can alleviate sweats by counteracting the chemicals that cause the blood vessels to expand, but it is far better to try to adapt to them using my more holistic approach. I do not advise reaching for the medicine cabinet immediately.

Treat yourself to a few specialized aromatherapy oils. The part of the brain that detects smell is closely linked with the emotional part of the brain. Oils are also absorbed into the skin and have powerful effects on the body. But you should always mix your chosen oil with a carrier oil, such as sweet almond, to prevent the undiluted essential oil irritating your skin. Good choices are:

- chamomile, which helps to relieve hot sweats and also has diuretic properties
- cypress, which helps relieve sweating and can also relieve vaginal dryness
- grapefruit, lemon and lime.

For those who prefer a herbal remedy, blackcurrant leaves are a good treatment for hot sweats, and a worthwhile homoeopathic treatment (available in tablet form from your chemist) is glonoin 30C, which should be taken

Simply

43

Radiant

every five minutes until the sweat recedes, for up to ten doses. Acupuncture has been known to help relieve hot sweats, and diet can also help alleviate symptoms. Eat more nuts, seeds, oily fish and wholegrain cereals. Avoid hot, spicy foods and limit your salt intake. Drink plenty of water as you are in danger of dehydrating.

Night Sweats

If you are experiencing hot sweats during the day, you may also suffer the discomfort of night sweats. You might wake up sweating profusely and feeling that you can't breathe. You might feel very hot or very cold, and find that having a wash doesn't help and you still can't sleep. In severe cases you might consider taking HRT as this can improve your quality of sleep, but one of the most useful solutions is to install an office fan by the side of your bed. You'll be amazed how much better you feel when you throw off the covers and let the cooling breeze blow across your body. Another good tip is to keep a bottle of chilled mineral water by the side of your bed to refresh you.

The herbal remedy horsetail, an ancient plant with jointed stems, which are dried, is a very good way to stop excessive night sweating. Or, before you go to bed, try making a bed-time drink from hot water, honey and three drops of essential oil of sage to reduce night sweats. Homoeopaths swear by sepia 6C tablets if you suffer profuse night sweats. You can take them hourly for up to ten doses.

FLUID RETENTION

Many women going through menopause suffer fluid retention, which can be extremely uncomfortable. The reason we can expect to gain weight and change shape during menopause is the fact that the body's chemical composition is changing quite rapidly and there is no time for the body's tissues to change with it. One of these changes is an increase in the amount of fatty tissue in your body. Because this tissue absorbs water you might develop the uncomfortable bulkiness of fluid retention, or bloating.

If you suffer from fluid retention, try the herbal remedy dandelion. It is widely used and has an excellent diuretic effect. A homoeopath's solution is apis 30C, especially if your fluid retention also involves restlessness and burning hot sweats. Bryonia 6C is a good choice, particularly if you also have painful breasts.

AVOIDING OSTEOPOROSIS

Osteoporosis, or brittle bone disease, is a silent killer. It is one of the most common conditions to affect post-menopausal women and is largely preventable, yet it has reached epidemic proportions in the Western world. More women die from hip fracture than from cancer of the ovary, uterus and cervix combined. By the age of 70, half of all women have dangerously brittle bones. What can you do to stop yourself becoming one of them?

Bone density reaches its peak at 35 to 40 and starts to decline when oestrogen levels begin to fall around the time of menopause. Don't delay: this is the time to take action, particularly if you prefer not to use HRT. If your teeth start to feel looser, do something about this today. The jaw bone is often first to be affected, but taking calcium supplements can help prevent the problem spreading. If you begin to take calcium early enough you may be able to meet your body's requirements without hormone therapy if you would prefer not to take it.

As a guide, you should take 1,500mg of calcium every day after the menopause, but this is achievable through a calcium sensitive diet, so you don't have to take supplements if you prefer not to. My recommendation is to sort the problem out by drinking an extra pint of skimmed or semi-skimmed milk every day, but if you can't eat dairy products you might need supplements. Other good sources of calcium are low-fat yogurt, tinned sardines and pilchards, parsley, leafy green vegetables such as

Did you know...

Reducing the amount you eat reduces the amount of nutrients available to your body. If you do not feel like eating large meals, make certain you choose foods containing pulses, nuts, wholegrains, fruit and vegetables.

Simply

45

Radiant

broccoli, spinach and watercress, dried figs, almonds, sesame seeds, Indian tea, nuts and seeds, curry powder, dry mustard, soya flour, self-raising flour, canned salmon and eggs.

To help protect yourself against osteoporosis, I also recommend eating a diet that is rich in essential fatty acids, which help your body retain calcium. The best sources are evening primrose oil and oily fish. Most nut oils (except peanuts) and dark green vegetables are also a good source.

OTHER WAYS TO MAINTAIN STRONG BONES

- Exercise strengthens bone, so keep moving.
- Thinning of the bones actually occurs mostly while you are lying down and the bones are not under pressure, so rise a little earlier each day to help counteract this process.
- Exposing your skin to a moderate amount of sunshine forms vitamin D in the skin, which helps your intestine to absorb calcium.

YOUR BODY'S SCENT

As we go through menopause, our hormone balance changes and this can affect our body's scent. Most women are not aware of this and, unfortunately, the change tends to be for the worse. An awareness of this is useful to our relationship with our partner. If you wear your normal perfume the action of the oils upon your skin may produce quite a different fragrance to the one you are used to, and it may be less attractive.

It is useful to change your perfume wearing habits at this stage of your life. My solution is to spray perfume lightly onto my clothes to maintain the scent that I am used to. This echoes something I have always done, and which my daughters have learned from me: spraying our favourite perfume on our pillows and bed linen. This smells so fresh and appealing, and creates a sensual environment for one's partner.

SLEEP

Sleep is a wonderfully inexpensive pleasure as well as being a very important part of the body's repair mechanism. It is the time when your body repairs tissue cells and when your mind sifts and sorts the subconscious superfluities of the day. Without enough sleep we are more prone to depression and less able to concentrate and make the right decisions about life. But although sleep is always vital to happy, healthy functioning, from mid-life onwards it is quite normal to need less. Try not to be troubled if you seem to be requiring less sleep as you grow older. Listen to your body. If you are tired, go to sleep, but don't worry if you still have plenty of energy but feel you ought to be going to sleep. Let your body provide the cues.

Research suggests that we produce less natural melatonin as we age. Since this is the hormone responsible for inducing sleepiness, it is likely that biochemically we will feel less inclined to sleep as we get older. It is quite normal for women to find as they age that their sleep needs reduce from nine hours a night to five or six. Try to see your decreased need for rest as an advantage and use the time gained on yourself: read a book, take a bath, give yourself a manicure, write a letter or be creative in another way.

But this doesn't mean you can't become sleep deprived in mid-life. Sleep studies have shown that women who experience hot sweats tend to have worse night-time sleep than those who do not and, frustratingly, this can make sufferers feel even more irritable and depressed. Listen to your body to assess your sleep needs, for it will always tell you if it is over-tired. Do you yawn too often? Are the muscles around your eyes tired? Do your legs feel weak?

The key is to be able to recognize when you are sleep deprived. If you fall into three or more of the following categories you might not be getting all the sleep you need.

+ You need an alarm clock in order to awake.
+ You feel tired and irritable during the week.
+ You have trouble concentrating or remembering.
+ You often fall asleep within five minutes of your head hitting the pillow.
+ You feel slow to solve problems or be creative.
+ You have dark circles around your eyes.
+ During the week you always hit the snooze button several times.
+ You feel drowsy when driving.
+ You often fall asleep watching television.
+ You believe you need a nap to make it through the day.
+ You struggle to get out of bed in the morning.
+ You sleep longer on weekend mornings.
+ You often fall asleep in meetings or lectures.
+ You often fall asleep after a heavy meal.

SLEEPING PILLS

It is best to avoid sleeping pills. Although they may knock you out you are likely to feel muzzy-headed the following day. Most types cause a reduction in the amount of Rapid Eye Movement, or REM, sleep in which dreams

Sleep is a very important part

occur. And if your natural ability to examine fears and concerns subconsciously through dreaming is interrupted you can end up feeling depressed. If you do use pills it is best to do so intermittently, so your body does not develop a dependency upon them. The best sort of pills are herbal slumber remedies, which work with your body to produce a natural sleep, rather than simply knock you out.

NATURAL SLEEP REMEDY

If you want a good night's sleep, avoid eating protein-rich foods after 6pm: they take much longer to digest. Hunger is a primitive alerting response, so the more hungry you are the more difficult it is to fall asleep. Aim to eat filling carbohydrates (such as potato, pasta, bread and cereals), which although heavy, are easily digested and will make you feel sleepy. And try to eat your evening meal before 7pm.

Make yourself a warm, milky drink just before you go to bed. Hot milk with cinnamon or nutmeg is a delicious alternative to hot chocolate, which contains caffeine and will keep you awake longer. But try not to drink too much in the evenings if you are having difficulty sleeping. A full bladder is guaranteed to interfere with your sleep.

Try to go to bed at the same time each night, and extend the ritual into a bed-time routine – brushing teeth, checking alarm clock etc. – that will set the mood for sleep. If you can't sleep, check your room isn't too hot. A temperature of 18–24 degrees is perfect for uninterrupted sleep: hotter or colder and you may find yourself waking.

Don't expect to fall asleep automatically if you are not physically tired. Physical exercise doesn't have to mean spending hours at the gym. Indulge in some gentle stretching exercises. Using your muscles will make sleep come more easily. Hold yourself in, tighten your buttocks, stretch

of the body's repair mechanism

your legs and arms. Arch your spine like a cat. Push your shoulders back and breathe deeply.

I'm a great believer in taking a bath at night as a holistic sleep enducer. Spend around 20 minutes in a lukewarm bath (If you have a sleeping problem and are taking a bath to relax never use water hot enough to make you sweat: this invigorates your circulation and keeps you awake. It also leads to premature skin deterioration, for skin cells age more quickly when the temperature of the body rises.) Light a candle, play some soothing music and burn incense if you have some. Use a favourite bubble bath or a few drops of an aromatherapy oil such as jasmine, lavender or neroli (the most expensive but most effective oil). A bath with liquid mineral salts or Dead Sea salts will encourage the elimination of waste through the skin, reduce fluid retention, smooth the skin and ease anxiety and stress. Do not read in the bath as this will keep your mind active. Instead think about becoming so relaxed that you will tumble into a delicious slumber after stepping from the water. Go to bed immediately after you've dried yourself and had a glass of cool water.

Make your bedroom your sanctuary for sleep and for sex. If you routinely use it to read, work, eat or watch television you are destroying the intimacy and quality of your retreat. If you awake in the night with a head running full of lists, get up and go into another room to make a list of all the issues on your mind. Once expelled on to paper you will have quietened the chattering mind and are likely to find that sleep will come much more easily once you return to your atmosphere of restful slumber.

Weight Gain

Like all women, you can expect to put on some weight as you approach the menopause. Your body, no longer involved in the monthly process of ripening an egg for possible fertilization, is changing chemically. You no longer have a fluctuating concentration of female hormone and this leads your body to slow down: your metabolic rate becomes more sluggish as you mature, and so you burn less energy more slowly. If your eating habits do not change and you do not increase the amount of exercise you take, then obviously you can expect to see changes in your physique. But these changes happen slowly. Often you don't realize your body has accumulated quite a bit of fat until, all of a sudden, an item of clothing no longer fits and you realize you have developed well-settled fat.

A common area in which to gain weight is on your hips and midriff. However, don't worry about a few extra pounds. A weight gain during menopause of seven to ten pounds is quite acceptable, and I believe should be left on the body. You are a wise, mature woman – love yourself for this healthy look. Far better to gracefully accept a certain weight gain

our metabolic rate slows as you mature

Did you know...

It is better to burn off excess calories through exercise than reduce the amount of nutrients consumed in your diet. Exercise also strengthens bones and muscles, and stimulates the brain with extra oxygen.

with age, rather than getting depressed about it and switching from one diet to another. People can become unhealthily obsessed with losing a half pound, but after a certain age it is not what you weigh on the scales that is relevant but what your measurements are. Keeping an eye on the proportion of fat on your frame is a much better guide. If you are piling on weight on your hips, for example, you may feel uncomfortable, but if your fat increases gently in proportion all over then you can look extremely attractive. Bear in mind that the average woman increases her body fat percentage from 27 per cent to 40 per cent between the ages of 25 and 70.

I have accepted that there is no way I will ever be slim. I was an 11 pound baby and have never been skinny. Because I am tall, when I was in my twenties I did look slim, but I always had fatty deposits and it has never bothered me. I put on weight when I had children. And following a car accident my physical activities became more limited, so I put on further weight. But I feel I am the right size for me. I feel confident, eat well and like myself, which is much more important than any textbook notions of 'correct' weight.

Remember, some slim bodies are ugly bodies. In my work I deal all day long with bodies and I encourage my clients to accept that they can deal with a certain amount of fat. The important thing is to enjoy your own touch. My advice is to stroke yourself all over your body. See if there is any part of it that you do not enjoy touching and concentrate on that area. You may find fat, or just as likely dry skin, scaly skin or spotty skin. Make a mental note to adopt a maintenance program for any area that particularly concerns you.

To maintain a dress size you are happy with, take up some gentle exercise. Rather than eating less you need to increase your metabolic rate by exercising more. Until now, running around the office, caring for children, or climbing up and down stairs might have been enough exercise to burn fat, but around the time of menopause the metabolic rate alters (as you age it does so by as much as three per cent per year) and you need to make more focused efforts to burn calories. Swimming, walking and golfing are all excellent gentle pursuits that will keep you in trim.

If you have decided you would like to lose a lot of weight, remember that after the age of 35 your face will be the first area to thin down, followed by your bust. Unfortunately the places where you actually want to lose weight – hips, bottom and thighs – are the last places to be affected by a diet program.

When you lose weight, lose it slowly so the skin has enough time to shrink with the underlying tissues. If you shed weight too rapidly the outer skin can be left looking a little on the large side and that can be difficult to correct. Some women then resort to the plastic surgeon, who can over-compensate, leaving the skin looking too tight. Far better to be lose weight slowly while enjoying the extra energy you'll have by not limiting yourself to starvation rations.

FOOD CRAVINGS

You might find you constantly feel hungry, even when you have just eaten. This is because the hormones that regulate appetite are confused by other falling hormone levels around the time of the menopause (this can also happen just before a period). Even though you've just eaten, you still feel hungry. The best way to control these cravings, which can lead you to eat up to 500 calories more than you need each day, is to snack on some carbohydrate, little and often. The best choice is a slice of wholemeal bread or a banana, this will also make you feel more cheerful and control any mood swings, but avoid carbohydrates that come with a bundle of extra fat, like doughnuts or sausage rolls. Chew slowly and pause between mouthfuls to offer your body the trigger that you are eating and would like to feel full.

If you still feel an urge to eat, drink a glass of fizzy water mixed with some lemon, or clean your teeth with a strongly flavoured tingling tooth-paste to signal to your stomach that no more food is forthcoming.

Still feeling hungry? It's time to ignore the feeling and go for a brisk walk. Redefine your eating patterns so that you eat a wholefood diet rich in fresh fruit and vegetables, and avoid sugar, which will increase your calories without making you feel full.

Even if you have never had a weight problem before menopause, you are likely to find that you have gained at least several pounds. Menopausal weight gain is a fact of life. Unfortunately, it is even more difficult to shed than the weight gained during pregnancy, but just as essential as the weight gained during puberty. It tends to show itself around the middle where you may notice an extra inch or two. Falling levels of oestrogen mean you start to store fat differently than when you were younger. Rather than gaining weight on breasts, hips and thighs, you might notice a more male pattern of weight gain, putting on weight around your abdomen. But don't view this as a complete excuse! One of the commonest causes is actually eating and drinking more than you now need. Female bodies are more efficient at using fuel than men and burn calories more slowly. And, as a woman ages, her energy requirements diminish. Therefore, leading a more sedentary lifestyle after your children leave home, or you retire, can decrease your daily energy requirement by up to half.

But there is also another reason for weight gain at this time of life. Hormonal changes at menopause actually change the function of your fat cells.

YOUR CHANGING FAT CELLS

Every woman's body contains around 30 billion fat cells. Unfortunately, fat cells have gender and a woman's fat cells are larger, more active and more resistant to dieting than a man's. Even more unfortunately, they become even larger and more stubborn during mid-life.

Females are more efficient at using

But, ironically, the very weight gain that disturbs us is actually for our advantage, according to Debra Waterhouse, an American nutrition expert and author of *Menopause Without Weight Gain*. She explains that although we might resent our fat cells, they have evolved a secondary function, contributing to our menopausal wellbeing as oestrogen-producing cells. When they detect falling oestrogen levels they increase their own production of the hormone, and this causes them to increase in size and number.

The fat cells in your waist grow the largest of all because they produce oestrogen more effectively than the fat cells in your thighs, buttocks and hips. The larger these midriff cells grow, the greater the physical benefits (fewer hot sweats, less intense PMS, improved sleep, milder mood swings). Consequently larger women have an easier menopausal transition than thin women. This can prove little comfort as most women are affected by the psychological burden of weight gain and its effect on body image.

Unfortunately, dieting doesn't help. These fat cells are tenacious in their mission to carry out their secondary function. Diets have close to a 100 per cent failure rate for menopausal women. Even on a restricted diet, they refuse to shrink and will fight back in their mission to ease your menopausal transition by producing the oestrogen you need.

But the good news is that it is possible to deal with this weight gain realistically. As your body is changing during menopause, your eating, exercise and lifestyle habits also need to evolve. My best advice here is don't fight your biology, instead learn to manage it.

The overall goal is to alter the way your fat cells function so that they store a bit less and release much more. Your fat cells expect you to diet and eagerly await your next bout of calorie deprivation. But when you eat regularly your fat cells start deactivating their fat storage enzymes. So the

Did you know...

Eating a little bit of a lot of things adds up to a balanced diet.

uel than men, burning calories slower

most effective way to trick your mid-life fat cells is never to diet again and eat instead when you are hungry.

Instead of skipping meals, eat five or six small meals a day. Don't over-eat when you do eat, eat moderately instead. Avoid eating the majority of your food intake at night, eat during the day instead. Remember: eating fat does not lead to weight gain unless you overeat.

And keep exercising. Not only will you burn calories, you will also change the way your body creates oestrogen, taking some of the pressure off those fat cell hormone factories. Researchers have discovered that exercise stimulates muscle cells to manufacture 25 per cent of the oestrogen your menopausal body needs. This enables the fat cells to shrink without compromising your health. Debra Waterhouse describes this as a 'win-win situation' and says, 'The more fit your muscles are, the less work your fat cells have to do, and the more co-operative they'll become in releasing fat.' Brilliant!

THE IMPORTANCE OF EXERCISE

Exercise is the best way to tackle weight gain at menopause, it costs nothing and has no negative side effects. Researchers at the Washington University School of Medicine studied a group of women throughout their menopause. Half the women exercised. The others did not. The findings make remarkable reading. Fit menopausal women had 13 per cent less body fat, were 26 pounds lighter and had four pounds more muscle.

Putting on only a few extra pounds can make it harder to get up from a sitting position, causing you to do less and walk more slowly. In turn, this can lead to more weight gain. Putting on 30 pounds over your ideal weight can place significant pressure on your knees, hips and lower spine. This can be painful, and the problem is compounded when you compensate by moving yet more slowly and doing even less.

If you are overweight, go on a sensible reduced eating plan, never a crash diet. Try to stick to around 1,000 calories a day. One of the disincentives for starving yourself, apart from the fact that it is bad for you, is that you will be unable to maintain it and when you return to a more normal eating pattern your body will already have compensated by slowing your metabolic rate. This means that eating just a normal quantity of food will make you even more susceptible to weight gain than you were before.

Whether you are trying to slim or not there are three eating rules you should try to adopt as you approach menopause.

1   **Increase your fibre intake:** This is a proven way of protecting against diabetes, high blood pressure and some types of cancer. Fibre-rich foods include: breakfast cereals, muesli, wholemeal (wholewheat) bread, oats, lentils, beans, spinach, cabbage and peas. Use wholemeal (wholewheat) flour for baking and leave the peel on potatoes and apples. Fibre absorbs water and helps beneficial bacteria grow in your gut. Your stools will be bulkier, providing exercise for your bowel.

2   **Cut down on the amount of salt you eat:** This lessens your chance of developing high blood pressure. Remember that processed foods often contain hidden amounts of salt, so try to look to more natural alternatives.

3   **Avoid an excess of fatty foods:** These are associated with diabetes, heart disease and some cancers, all of which you are more susceptible to as you mature. But at no point should you eat a completely fat-free diet. That is one of the biggest mistakes people make. We need a certain amount of fat to keep our body functioning effectively. Continue to dress your salads and cook in vegetable oil: the best is olive oil, instead of butter, or use ghee – the Indian equivalent.

Did you know...

Iron is needed by red blood cells before they can carry oxygen around the body. It is found in leafy-green vegetables, egg yolk, red meat and fortified cereals,

Did you know...

The cholesterol in your diet has little effect on the level of cholesterol in your blood. Doctors believe the levels of saturated fat in food is a more important factor.

You need to move during your mid-life years more than ever before. Your menopausal body depends upon exercise to:

Fight fatigue: Menopausal women who exercise regularly report 25 per cent more energy than those who do not.

Recharge your metabolism: Exercise can boost metabolism by up to eight per cent, allowing you to eat the same number of calories at age 50 as you did at age 30.

Reduce mental sluggishness: When you are fit you think more clearly and react faster mentally.

Stabilize your moods: Exercise releases serotonin and the endorphins – the brain chemicals that naturally affect mood. Fit menopausal women are significantly less depressed and anxious and are affected less by mood swings.

Reduce food cravings: Menopausal women who exercise report 39 per cent fewer fat cravings and 22 per cent fewer sugar cravings. Fitness is so satisfying to your body that you will even find that fatty, sweet foods become less appetizing.

Reduce hot sweats: Exercise helps your body to metabolize heat-producing hormones and can reduce hot sweats by up to 50 per cent. The average sedentary menopausal woman experiences 15 hot sweats a day, compared to eight for an active menopausal woman.

Strengthen your bones: Researchers have found that fit women maintain bone density throughout mid-life, while sedentary women lose at least one per cent a year.

Reduce your risk of breast cancer: Postmenopausal women who exercised for at least four hours a week had a 37 per cent lower risk of breast cancer.

Reduce your risk of heart disease: A study of 73,000 women showed that as activity level increased, heart disease risk decreased.

Live longer: As little as one hour of exercise a week reduces the risk of death by 24 per cent.

Did you know...

Copper, found in nuts, seeds and cocoa, works with many natural processes that block the damaging effects of free radicals.

59

Simply

Radiant

Cellulite is the by-product of a system

Cellulite

Cellulite is stubborn and sexist. But it is often viewed as an *inevitable* curse of being female. It doesn't have to be that way. If you aim to avoid an unhealthy diet, sedentary lifestyle and poor circulation, you can help yourself avoid the toxic sludge that is cellulite. It is a myth that only fat women suffer. As long as 25 years ago, studies showed that people existing on the average Western diet were seriously deficient in many important nutrients – a major cause of cellulite. Unfortunately, playing on our insecurities about body image, all sorts of bogus treatments have been suggested to treat the bumpy, dimpled deposits that are still often misunderstood as fat.

Cellulite is the hard, lumpy, dimpled 'orange-peel' effect that appears on upper arms, bottoms and thighs. It is waste that has become trapped in fat cells directly beneath the skin and is the by-product of a system that is trying to maintain our health. One of the body's most effective mechanisms for protecting itself from toxins taken in through food is to lock them in fat cells, encasing them in fluid and binding them up with hardened connective tissue. This is a peculiarly female affliction. Men just don't tend to

Did you know...

A headache may be telling you to enjoy a drink of water or juice. At these times, avoid tea and coffee. The caffeine they contain acts as a mild diuretic and encourages the body to flush out more fluids.

that is trying to maintain our health

suffer from cellulite because their skin and underlying tissues are constructed differently.

So what can women do to gain the upper hand in the war against cellulite? Arm ourselves with correct information to start with. Cellulite is visual evidence that there is waste from the metabolic process left in the body. People sometimes imagine that their cellulite has developed overnight, but it is actually a slow process that occurs over many years. Many women with cellulite have a history of crash dieting and rapid weight gain, which leads toxic deposits to build up a bit like the sludge on a river bed, and they cause the puckered thighs and dimpled bottoms of cellulite sufferers. The good news is that you can arrest its development, but you would be unwise to expect a miracle. If you try to banish it too fast, it will return twice as fast. You can't walk into a clinic and imagine that money will buy you an intensive week-long treatment of cellulite removal. Instead, you need a longer-term perspective. Look for a light, sustainable treatment that you can carry out at home, or with a professional therapist on a weekly basis.

The proof is in the pudding. If you embark on an anti-cellulite regime you will discover that cellulite is not an unaesthetic genetic legacy and it doesn't have to be 'just part of being a woman'. The deposits of waste material that settle around certain large muscles really can be reduced in area and intensity.

There are three processes that, when used together over a period of time, can achieve these results: a detoxifying diet; regular body polishing to stimulate the circulation using a woman's greatest beauty tool, her hands; and lymphatic drainage massage upon the bulges. This regime doesn't have to cost a fortune, and it doesn't have to take up a lot of time. A few minutes a day, every day, should produce visible results after about a month.

The main causes of cellulite are an

Although visiting a skilled professional therapist is an effective solution, it is perfectly possible to develop your own home-care treatment regime once you understand the principles underlying your mission and find the will to invest some time in changing your shape to improve your self esteem. Why consider uncomfortable, expensive, potentially dangerous surgery when there are methods of helping the toxins melt away harmlessly? The combination of the right diet, massage and the correct essential oils means that unsightly pockets of fat can be eradicated forever.

In order to help prevent your thighs and bottom from continuing to develop that unappealing overstuffed 'orange-peel' look as you get older, it helps to understand what cellulite really is and what you can really do to shift it without wasting a lot of time and energy on treatments that are destined to fail. Cellulite is sophisticated. It is caused by eating the wrong kinds of food and living the wrong kind of lifestyle, rather than simply eating too much or taking too little exercise. So more exercise and eating less cannot, by themselves, solve the problem.

Deposits of cellulite are actually reserves of liquid toxic waste that the body is unable to expel by normal means. The liver is your body's filtration system, but when it is overloaded, some toxins remain in the body rather than being processed. Initially, areas of cellulite are soft because they consist of waterlogged cells, but as cellulite gradually accumulates as the years go by it becomes progressively harder and more grainy. This makes it more difficult to remove, but it is never impossible to budge.

As women age, the problem tends to become worse as even more polluted fluid accumulates around the capillaries supplying individual fat cells in the thighs and bottom. Unfortunately, wherever you already have some cellulite, conditions are always perfect for more to form. So there is no time like the present to start the process of shifting what you have already accumulated.

Did you know...

Manganese, a vital mineral micronutrient, is needed for the production of energy and the maintenance of healthy bones and connective tissue. Healthy connective tissue keeps skin firm. Life-bearing foods are good sources of manganese.

unhealthy diet and sedentary lifestyle

The presence of cellulite is nothing to do with being overweight. Instead it shows that your body's internal balance is disturbed. You can be verging on anorexia and still have cellulite. Or you can be extremely overweight and have smooth, unblemished thighs. You do not gain fat because the liver is not functioning properly. Fat shows that your general digestive system is sluggish and fat alone will never cause the unaesthetic, bumpy appearance of cellulite. The dreaded orange peel effect occurs when the cells cannot move freely and are trapped in connective tissue, feeling hard and knobbly, rather than soft and malleable like ordinary fat areas. Whatever your shape you need to read cellulite as a visual indication that your body needs a thorough overhaul, cleanse and detoxification.

For years, the vast majority of British and American doctors denied the existence of cellulite, refusing to accept that women have a special sort of fat and insisting that cellulite is an invention of cosmetic companies wishing to sell products. Recently, however, a number of British dermatologists have conducted research that has gone some way to narrowing the gap between Britain and France. For nearly fifty years French doctors have accepted cellulite as a genuine medical affliction. Because they believe it is caused by the action of female hormones on water and body wastes, which can lead to more serious afflictions, such as arthritis or permanent water retention, they even offer anti-cellulite treatments on their equivalent of the National Health Service. The French are enlightened. Arthritis can be caused when a high concentration of acidic waste toxins in the body dissolve connective tissue.

THE ROLE OF OESTROGEN IN THE FORMATION OF CELLULITE

The catalyst for the production of cellulite is oestrogen, which performs a protective as well as reproductive function in our bodies. The more oestrogen in a woman's body, the more likely that she will develop cellulite, particularly if she has poor circulation. Oestrogen predisposes women towards retaining fluid, and one of its protective tasks is to send toxins away from vital organs to low-risk areas – thighs, buttocks, upper arms – and wrap these poisons safely away in fatty deposits to prepare the body for pregnancy. This explains why women are afflicted by cellulite and men are not. Men's bodies deal with toxins in a more global, diffuse way; their arteries fur up. While this may have the advantage of being invisible it is, unlike cellulite, extremely dangerous.

But why aren't our bodies more efficient at dispelling redundant toxins from food, rather than simply moving them around? The answer is that although we have evolved a system for this, it has been overloaded by our modern lifestyle. Too many processed foods, prescription drugs, a sluggish lymphatic system (see below), coffee, alcohol, cigarettes and pesticides alter our hormonal balance and toxins are produced. The body copes as best it can to expel the unwanted material produced by these substances, but any excess is dumped in outlying body areas. The body then makes no further attempt to expel them considering it has done its job of protecting us.

The Key Causes of Cellulite

Cellulite is caused mainly by leading an unhealthy lifestyle. Oestrogen cannot send anti-nutrients to outlying areas unless there is rubbish to send. These are the substances to cut out if you wish to help prevent cellulite from forming:

COFFEE

More than three cups of coffee a day can contribute to the formation of cellulite. Caffeine is the most harmful of all cellulite-causing substances. It puts extra stress on the adrenal glands, which release adrenaline we do not need. Adrenaline exists to give us a sudden energy boost in case of danger, but caffeine enables this hormone to be secreted constantly, causing clogging. For most women, cellulite is an indicator they are eating too much chocolate, or drinking too much coffee, tea (which has half the amount of caffeine found in coffee) or fizzy drinks.

NICOTINE

A woman's system is less able than a man's to withstand the poisons released by tobacco in the blood-stream. Nicotine competes with the red blood cells to pick up oxygen in the lungs. This means that every cell in the body receives less oxygen than it should. This is relevant to the formation of cellulite because oxygen acts as a powerful blood cleanser, so as well as adding to the toxic waste in the body, smoking also reduces our ability to deal with it.

ALCOHOL

Our bodies have a full-time job handling ordinary waste materials produced by our diet. When we drink alcohol, women's livers and kidneys, which are smaller than men's, cannot effectively handle the excess waste material. Much of the waste matter stays in the system to be shunted out of harm's reach.

THE WRONG FOODS

Few women eating wholefoods, lots of fruit and vegetables and avoiding tea, coffee and alcohol develop a cellulite problem. But the artificial, saturated-fat diet enjoyed in the West creates eliminative difficulties for our bodies. Cellulite is always worst in countries where saturated fats form a significant part of the diet. Indian women tend to suffer far less than Western women, even those of us who are on the ample side.

The more natural the food the quicker the digestive system breaks it down, but the more synthetic the food is the longer it takes to be processed by the body. Waste material that is not broken down is reabsorbed back into the body where it starts to do damage. When too much accumulates our system clogs up, circulation becomes sluggish and cellulite begins to form.

Avoid eating sugar (which has a similar effect on the body as caffeine, and creates an overproduction of adrenaline), dairy products (which are mucus-forming and encourage waste material to become sticky and stay in the body), meat (which takes a long time to be digested by the body) and anything processed, smoked or preserved (many food additives are often difficult for our system to expel effectively).

INACTIVITY

Sitting at a desk all day long can impair our circulation. Is it so surprising then that when treating cellulite I often notice that particularly intense areas form where my clients' legs meet their chair edge at work? Inactivity leads to a sluggish circulation, which makes the blood and lymphatic system tasks even more difficult.

THE ROLE OF THE LYMPHATIC SYSTEM

There are two types of fluid that work to carry excess body wastes away: blood and lymph. Lymph is similar to blood except it is colourless, containing no red blood cells. One of the most important elements of a healthy body is to have a correctly functioning lymphatic system. Lymph vessels are found in every cell. Their role is to pump waste matter from the cells into the blood stream through valves made of muscle tissue. When oestrogen sends impurities away from vital organs into other cells of the body, a healthy lymphatic system will in turn attempt to drain these cells, as it does all over the body, but when the lymph vessels are sluggish, the waste stays and accumulates. When there is a build-up of mucoid matter the lymphatic system cannot drain the cells efficiently and the result is congestion. The first step in getting rid of cellulite is to cleanse the lymphatic system. The best way to do this is to eat a diet that excludes foods that form this cell clogging mucus (see below).

Did you know...

Fruit and vegetables supply about 20 per cent of the water we consume? Melon and juicy vegetables – like tomatoes and cucumbers – are good sources of water.

THE ANTI-CELLULITE SOLUTION

The key to reducing cellulite is a combination of several processes used consistently. Nothing will work if used only occasionally. And there is no point being dedicated to the routine I outline below and then drinking a lot of alcohol. You are trying to help your liver – your body's filtration organ – to function more efficiently at removing toxins, so don't give it extra work to do.

Before starting your bid to reduce your cellulite, you might wish to measure your thighs at the thickest point and take a note of the measurement. Then as you conduct the programme measure your thighs on a weekly basis. If you are dedicated you should see a measurable reduction in the size of your thighs after about a month.

DIET

What you eat is the most important component of a reduced-cellulite physique. Diet is a vital component, not an optional extra. And however effective you are in shifting the cellulite you have it is likely to return unless you change your eating habits. Eliminate all highly-processed and junk food from your kitchen. Dispose of bread made from refined flour, boxed breakfast cereals, white pasta and white sugar (often found as a cheap bulking agent in processed food such as baked beans). Up your intake of salad: try to eat at least one tasty salad a day and remember to chew all food thoroughly. An anti-cellulite diet has a two-fold effect. Firstly, it helps detoxify the system, making it more effective at eliminating toxic build up. Secondly, by reducing the amount of impurities you eat you can limit the future formation of more cellulite.

A natural, wholefood diet is the best way of gradually enabling the body to rid itself of accumulated toxins. Certain foods linger too long in the colon and can begin to start decomposing before being expelled, leading to the production of toxins that can contribute to the formation of cellulite. The key is to eat foods that are easily digested and pass swiftly through the system. And to avoid milk and dairy products, which slow down digestion by forming mucus, a sticky substance that clogs the digestive tract and blocks up the lymphatic drainage system.

To give your cellulite detoxification program a jump start, cut out all wheat and dairy products for three months. For the first few days eat only fruit every two hours (avoiding citrus which can aggravate the liver). You can eat up to six pounds of fruit a day, but try to eat only one type of fruit at each sitting. Bananas, apples, pears, pineapple, strawberries, raspberries, grapes, mango, papaya and kiwi fruit are very beneficial.

Drink mineral water throughout, and abstain from stimulants such as coffee and tea. I'm a great believer in drinking hot water first thing in the morning, but you can add lemon to taste if you need it. It is excellent for clearing the alimentary canal and dissolving fatty deposits as well as aiding digestion and constipation.

You can then modify the diet by introducing simple, unprocessed food. Good lymph-clearing foods are fresh fruit and vegetables, organic if possible. Potatoes, spinach, celery, carrots, green peppers, swedes (rutabaga) and beans are all good when cooked, and the portions can be as large as you like. Spinach, cauliflower and broccoli are excellent eaten raw with minimal lemon dressing. Eat wholegrains such as brown rice and millet, wheatbran and oatbran, but fish, eggs and lean meat should be eaten only sparingly. Substitute tea, coffee and alcohol with herb teas and fruit juices.

This anti-cellulite eating plan is not designed to help you lose weight. You may become slimmer, but this is not the express purpose here. The diet is focused upon encouraging long-held body wastes to disperse. It is a healthy and potent body-cleansing system.

WATER

One of the most effective treatments for cellulite is as simple as life itself: water. Drinking plenty of it is a must. If you have a cellulite tendency remember that 70 per cent of the human body is made up of water, forming a rich soup full of chemicals and minerals. In the average person there are five litres of water in the blood, and five more in the lymphatic system, digestive juices and other secretions. When you drink a lot of water you encourage the whole system to flush itself out in a water exchange that will loosen the fat cells and toxins that contribute to cellulite. People mistakenly believe that fizzy drinks, fruit juice and tea can do much the same job as water, but they don't because they require processing by the body. Only water can successfully rehydrate the body and cleanse the system.

If you suffer from cellulite try to drink at least one litre of water a day, but there is no point downing it all in the morning, because you will end up in the bathroom. Far better to keep a glass of water beside you all day and sip intermittently – you'll be surprised how easy it is to drink a healthy, cellulite-busting amount.

LYMPHATIC DRAINAGE MASSAGE

This is one of my core philosophies in the bid to shift cellulite. There is no lotion or unguent on the market that can melt away cellulite: you can't tone up flabby areas and improve your contours by smearing on a cream. Nothing can make cellulite go away except hard work. But an intensive lymphatic drainage massage, professional or self-administered, is very effective when used in combination with the right diet.

Lymphatic drainage is a pain-free, but vigorous, pummelling massage, focused specifically upon areas of cellulite build-up, that loosens the build up of toxins. It also activates the lymph nodes, helping to transport the toxins away from the affected area. Aromatherapy oils such as lemon, frankincense, juniper, black pepper and sandalwood are my preference during a lymphatic drainage massage. These oils are not just pleasing scents, they also have an extremely effective detoxifying effect, enabling waste matter to leave the cells and pass into the lymphatic system.

After body polishing (*see below*) take a bath and add a few drops of your chosen oil to the water. Pummel and knead the cellulite heavy areas. After you have finished bathing, massage a diluted droplet of the oil into your thigh and buttocks. The oils will take about ten minutes to be completely absorbed.

After you have pummelled your cellulite you can begin to activate your lymph nodes. Although only a professional therapist can give a complete lymphatic drainage session, you can learn for yourself where your lymph nodes are and press these after you have finished your pounding massage. Touching the nodes under the armpits, the groin and behind the knees can aid the functioning of your lymphatic system. Apply gentle pressure until any tenderness ceases.

At first, follow this routine every day. After three or four weeks use the oils every other day. When you can see a noticeable change in your cellulite you can cut down to once or twice a week. But remember: you will see no change if you don't also alter your eating habits.

BODY POLISHING

In other books, this is the point when therapists mention 'body brushing'. This is a fairly strenuous, dry-friction technique, which can damage the capillaries when women become over-enthusiastic. I do not endorse or practise it. Instead, I advocate body polishing, or what I call 'palm and finger gliding'. This is a mild form of acupressure administered with the hands, which is an effective way of clearing and cleansing the lymphatic system, and also removes any dead cells, leaving the skin feeling soft. It is far more natural to use your own hands rather than a scratchy brush. Polishing skin with your hands stimulates the expulsion of stagnant accumulations of waste material that are obstructing your lymphatic system.

Start palm and finger gliding at the same time you begin your new eating plan. You should spend five minutes a day, and to be effective should do so for several months. But don't confine yourself only to areas of cellulite. Circulation is a whole body process.

Polishing should never be done on dry skin. Instead, moisten your hands with water. The strokes you use should be light, long and even, with the full palm; fingers and thumb in contact with your skin. Without damaging the blood vessels you will be loosening the fat. Place the palms of your hands flat against your skin and let them follow every contour, gliding the fingers behind. This is not at all strenuous. First, polish up the back of the leg in long strokes. At the thigh, stroke repeatedly to shift the stubborn areas of accumulated toxins within the cellulite. Palming the buttocks in a circular direction is also an effective way of reducing your tendency to form pimples, which are caused by follicles becoming irritated from a lot of sitting down. Then move on to the front of your thighs, followed by arms, torso and neck. When you have finished step into a warm bath. This routine is a stress-reducing therapy in itself.

THE BENEFITS OF DEEP BREATHING
A stressful lifestyle is often run on adrenaline. Unfortunately, adrenaline is one of the toxic elements that can lead to the formation of

cellulite when the liver is unable to filter excess quantities from the blood. Reducing the amount of stress and anxiety in your life is one way to limit the production of adrenaline, so try to practise deep breathing whenever possible. Take time in the bath, or when lying in bed to take large breaths, which will help boost your oxygen levels, improve your circulation and calm you down. See page 41 for the Stress Buster exercise, to practise deep breathing.

I am also a great advocate of the benefits of simply sitting still as a method of giving your body and mind a chance to relax and refresh. It takes a few minutes at most and costs nothing. Try it several times a day to help stressful feelings drain away. And as for those doubters who insist that cellulite is a permanent feature of their physical landscape that no amount of pummelling will shift, remember that the most important part of you is the part that is on the inside.

ALGAE AND SEAWEED SOLUTIONS

The sea yields several substances that are good armaments in the face of encroaching cellulite. All seaweeds, from kelp to Japanese nori are rich in trace elements and minerals, which aid the body's metabolic function, and are an extremely rich source of calcium. The more sea plants you can incorporate into your diet the better. Seaweed fibre can bind and remove waste materials from the body and is a good detoxifier for cellulite-prone women. Spirulina is a fresh water algae and has the richest iron content known to nature, more vitamin E than wheatgerm and up to six times as much vitamin B12 as raw beef. It is a good nutritional supplement to take if you suffer from cellulite. Take tablets or buy spirulina powder and make it into a hot drink, mixed with a light vegetable soup.

Stress, pollution, poor nutrition and

Hair

A robust head of hair is truly a woman's crowning glory and the perfect barometer of her health. When your hair is clean, shiny, lustrous, thick, well-nourished and well-styled you feel confident and capable, but a bad hair day diminishes our mood and takes away our sparkle. Hair continuously goes through growth and resting periods, and lack-lustre locks denote stress and an inadequate diet. You produce seven miles of hair a year, and it needs care whatever your age. Today, more than ever, the odds are against us. Stress, pollution, poor nutrition, excessive styling, sunbathing, lack of exercise, and chemicals and dyes all fight against our chances of healthy hair. Unfortunately my experience with clients has shown me that during menopause hair loss can increase to varying degrees.

Most women agree that when their hair starts to fall out their confidence disappears at the same rate. This is regrettable because there is a direct link between stress, depression and hair loss. Worrying about it can actually

styling all actively damage our hair

increase the problem. But bear in mind that in your forties, the hair shaft decreases in diameter, so hair that feels like it is thinning could actually just be getting finer. Well-layered, shorter cuts show off fine hair to its full advantage.

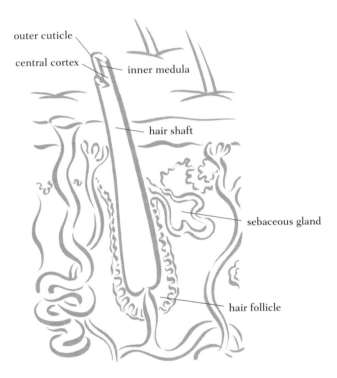

outer cuticle

central cortex — inner medula

hair shaft

sebaceous gland

hair follicle

cross section of hair

The lack of oestrogen, combined with the natural changes your body undergoes as you get older, can make your hair feel drier, coarser and more brittle than usual. If this is happening to you, or if your hair seems to be accelerating in its greyness, then increase your intake of essential fatty acids. Also, take a daily dose of evening primrose oil, a fish oil, and consider a course of multivitamins that will provide nourishment.

HAIR LOSS

You are brushing your hair one day when the brush seems to be completely clogged with strands of hair. You simply do not lose that amount of hair on a daily basis, and you gaze at the strands running a distressing calculation through your head ... try not to worry. The average head carries between 100,000 and 150,000 hairs, so you can afford to lose plenty every day. Hair thins from 50, but treated with care it can look lustrous even beyond that milestone. But some women do suffer from something similar to male pattern hair loss as they go through menopause. It is usually caused by changing hormone levels, which mean that the small amount of testosterone all healthy women produce is getting the upper hand. Women also lose hair on the crown or at their temples because stress increases levels of male hormones. You can ask your doctor for progesterone supplements if you are very troubled. Equally, if you lose significant amounts of hair you might be one of the minority who develop alopecia, a hair loss disorder that can cause hair to fall out in clumps, and you should definitely consult your doctor for advice.

Scientists are now developing a greater understanding of the causes of hair loss. A research team at London's St Thomas' Hospital has traced a link between the thymus gland and hair loss. They have found that the rate at which we lose hair increases in accordance with decreases in levels of the hormone thymolin. This tends to happen at times of physical and emotional stress. Diet is a key factor in preventing thinning. Stick to healthy foods and avoid processed alternatives, and up your intake of fruit and vegetables to give your follicles the nutrients they need to keep your hair in place. However much you condition your hair, remember that the roots are the most important part, because that is where the hair is alive and growing. Like a plant, the hair is governed by its roots, so eat well. A good breakfast is vital. Some foods, like cheese, can take around four

Did you know...

Your hair tells the world how healthy you are. Include nuts and oily fish, pumpkin seeds and red meat, apricots and green leafy vegetables in your diet for strong and shiny hair.

Simply

77

Radiant

hours to digest, so by the time their nourishment reaches the hair follicles it is more than 12 hours since they last obtained nutrients.

Millet is a useful food for promoting healthy, lustrous hair. It contains seven of the eight amino acids your hair needs, as well as being high in growth-promoting vitamin B. Stir millet flakes into muesli, or use it instead of rice and pasta.

DANDRUFF, SCALING AND DULL HAIR

For hair problems such as these, the B vitamin group and brewers' yeast are great preventatives, while olive or coconut oils, cod-liver oil, almonds and sunflower and pumpkin seeds give you a glossy, Mediterranean shine. To strengthen the shaft of your newly-growing hair, you need a high-protein diet. Seaweed too helps to keep hair growing, so ask for spirulina, a concentrated seaweed tablet, at your local health food shop.

A good homoeopathic remedy is rekevic, which gives hair an extra boost. Combine it with foods high in iron and vitamins, like green vegetables and liver, for increasing the speed of your hair growth. Drinking plenty of water will also really make a difference to the condition of your hair. But no matter how well you eat, bad habits like smoking and drinking to excess will close down your capillaries and cut off the blood supply to the roots of your hair.

Head massage is an excellent way of improving blood supply to hair follicles, nourishing the roots and increasing the growth rate. If your scalp feels spongy you may have a stagnation similar to cellulite, caused by sluggish circulation. As we get older, our circulation slows down and the hair can thin. You can do much to alleviate this by massaging your scalp once a week when applying shampoo. Head massage works by stimulating the

To strengthen new hair growth

follicles and increasing the blood supply. Plant your ten fingers over the crown of the head, make finger balls (*see page 122*) and work your way down the back of your scalp, applying deep pressure. Then place your fingers at the base of your head. Spend a few minutes working your fingers thoroughly over your head, and make this routine a way of life. Within a few weeks formerly limp hair will bounce back because of the invigorated circulation feeding the follicle.

Good brushing completes the process by smoothing down the hair follicles on each hair shaft. Always use a wide, blunt-toothed brush and never pull at tangles. If your hair is still insistent on splitting, have it cut every eight weeks. Cut off just half an inch, so you are going two steps forward and one step back.

UNWANTED HAIR

Changing hormone levels at menopause can lead to the development of facial and body hair. This can be particularly confidence shattering. I treat many professional women who have spent their lives consumed by work. There comes a time when they begin to crave a long-lasting relationship. They are interesting, successful, financially independent, but their self esteem is being eroded by the emergence of a couple of unwanted hairs. Don't suffer in silence. If you have unwanted hair in an unusual location you can guarantee you are not the first. The problem can be fairly easily corrected.

When you notice fine hairs growing on your face – or even longer, blacker more obvious hairs – the temptation is to become quite distressed. At a point in your life while your femininity already seems compromised, you now seem to be growing a beard. Try not to despair. Excess hair is

you need a high-protein diet

quite common. Twenty five per cent of women have noticeable hair on their face, 15 per cent on their chest, 30 per cent on their tummy and 40 per cent on their thighs.

The reason for this is the male hormone testosterone. All healthy women produce small amounts of this chemical, but its influence is normally obscured by oestrogen. When oestrogen levels begin to fall around the time of menopause, the male hormone has a chance to make its influence felt. As a result, facial hair increases. By the age of 65, four women in every ten have a moustache.

The best way to cope is by using depilatory creams, plucking, waxing or epilation. If you can afford it, and are sufficiently concerned, a course of electrolysis, which is pain-free but expensive, is the only way to permanently remove hair, although it can take several courses of treatment to achieve this. The key aspect is to avoid scarring, and before you go ahead with a salon treatment discuss this with them. Scar tissue can be more unsightly and upsetting than unwanted hair, particularly on the upper lip. Shaving doesn't make hair thicker or encourage it to grow faster. But it does slice hair at an angle that means it soon becomes more noticeable again.

Did you know...

Coarse hair and dry skin may be signs of low iodine levels in the diet. Lowered iodine also lead to a lack of energy. Good sources of this essential mineral micronutrient include: iodised salt, seafood and seaweed. A feeling of apathy can mean you should eat more iodine-rich foods.

TINTING

With age, pigment production slows down, leading to greying. If you go grey and you don't appreciate the look then consider tinting your hair. This can give you a massive boost of confidence, particularly if you are greying prematurely. If I don't tint my hair I'm completely grey, but no-one would ever know because I never let even the slightest hint of my roots show. I use professional dye once a fortnight at home. Ask your hair colourist to tell you what they are using and apply it wearing plastic gloves. Vegetable dyes provide the most natural cover for grey hair, and the best effect is obtained with a dye a shade lighter than your own.

10 STEPS TO THE PERFECT HAIR WASH

1   Brush your hair before washing to free loose hair.
2   Wet hair very thoroughly.
3   Apply a dollop of shampoo the size of a 50 pence coin. Choose a shampoo geared towards the condition of your scalp, not your hair. You want to use a gentle shampoo that will not strip your scalp of its oil in the bid to clean greasy hair.
4   Massage your scalp gently – rubbing roughly over-activates the sebaceous glands, and hair will look greasy more quickly. Leave your shampoo in your hair for 10 minutes before rinsing with copious warm water.
5   Apply conditioner to the ends, not the roots, and comb it through the hair with a wide-toothed comb, taking care not to stretch the hair as this will make it more inclined to break when it dries. Never brush your hair when it is wet. For a truly resplendent mane, you must use just the right amount of conditioner. Too much leaves hair lank, and too little leaves it parched.
6   Start combing hair at the ends and inch your way towards the roots, holding the hair in small bunches and cautiously teasing the comb through it.
7   Keep rinsing with lashings of water that is not too hot.
8   Don't tangle hair by rubbing it dry or wrapping it in a turban towel. Lightly wring out any excess water.
9   Leave it to dry naturally if you can. If you must blow dry use a diffuser to minimize heat damage.
10   When your hair is dry, rub a tiny dash of coconut oil vigorously between your palms to heat it up and smooth your fingers over your hair. This will give a beautiful shine and attractive scent.

OILING

Hair can look rather limp and dull during menopause. If the digestive system isn't working properly the most visibly affected areas are hair and nails, which rely upon keratin, a protein that holds onto moisture. When that protein is reduced the moisture levels in skin and hair fall and you can become more prone to splitting and dryness. So to keep hair nice and shiny I recommend oiling the hair with coconut oil, which is inexpensive and smells wonderful. Comb a small amount through your hair, from roots to ends, and leave overnight for a glossy head of hair. As the oil can be very greasy, use it sparingly on the scalp itself. You may need to wash your hair thoroughly the following morning. You could also try olive oil as an intensive conditioner and peachnut oil for added shine.

Skin

When you were a child your skin fitted you perfectly. It was taut, yet beautifully elastic and flexible, moulding perfectly to your contours as you moved and played. But as the years pass, and it is constantly exposed to the weather, and endlessly bent and folded and stretched, it begins to show some signs of wear. Yet it is astonishing just how resilient skin is given its incredible thinness – between 15 and 21 thousandths of an inch thick – and amazing that it doesn't show some signs of deterioration much much earlier.

As you age your skin will change, that much is inevitable. However, if you take the time to care for your skin you can do a great deal to limit the extent of these visible signs and continue to present a confident face to the world: a face of which you are proud, that reflects the person you know you are on the inside with all that accumulated confidence and wisdom. Feeling good is often directly connected to a positive self image. Why surrender your appearance – and your mood – to the passage of time when you don't have to? Start early enough, and you can sustain a youthful appearance from 30 to 55, for these are the years in which physical

our metabolic rate slows as you mature

changes can be most easily controlled. But irrespective of how many changes you can already see, there is much you can do to slow future visible deterioration with the knowledge I will share. Whatever your age, you can halt the speed of future changes with my common sense beauty routines.

Your skin's appearance is affected by your lifestyle, diet and environment. The surface of your body is a visual barometer for the strains you place upon your body in general. Factors such as stress, lack of sleep, fast foods, harsh weather and pollution all take a heavy toll. The result is often a dull complexion, spots, premature wrinkles and dry, flaky skin. Although these problems are usually most severe on the face – the primary exposed area and the first to show signs of age – you can do much to alleviate them once you become aware that many of these visible changes can be exacerbated by poor circulation. This leads to stagnation in the skin and an inability to expel blockages from the cuticles.

Picture a bowl of water. If it is left to stand it will inevitably start to stagnate, but run water through the bowl of water and it will remain fresh. Our skin is the same. Drinking water and eating nutrient-rich food will nourish your body's tissues and help waste toxins to pass through, rather than accumulate. In the Western world, we don't drink nearly enough water to flush out the impurities and toxins we digest; water is the most important component of looking beautiful. Improving your circulation and lymph system are the keys to minimizing stagnation, for reduced blood flow through your skin's capillaries reduces the nutrients your skin receives and impairs the efficient removal of metabolic wastes. If your circulation is poor, you will be able to read this in your skin. Your skin will gradually become thinner, less elastic, and fine lines will appear, leading eventually to full-blown wrinkles.

Changes in the texture of a woman's skin begin on average before her thirtieth birthday. But the natural deterioration of the skin begins earlier, in our twenties, before there are any visible clues. The first clues you do

Simply Radiant

Did you know...
Scientists believe beta-carotene is a powerful antioxidant that fights skin wrinkles caused by free radical damage, and protects against heart disease and certain cancers. However, beta-carotene needs to work with other natural substances in food to be effective, so choose a well rounded diet combining red and orange foods with life-bearing foods.

see are very subtle; smile lines emerge, as does a tiny horizontal fold of extra skin beneath the eyes and a very minor bagging of the upper eyelid. As time passes, the smile lines become longer and more deeply incised, remaining etched upon your face even when you are no longer smiling. Your upper eyelids begin to look slightly puffy. You notice that it is becoming harder to apply eye-makeup smoothly without the skin bunching up beneath the applicator slightly. As time marches on, the line from outside your nostril to the corner of your mouth becomes more deeply incised, frown lines between the eyebrows are more obviously etched, lines begin to work their way into your skin downwards from the corners of your mouth, eye bags become more permanent, upper-eyelid skin becomes more hooded, making you look tired even if you have slept well, small pockets of fat accumulate in the lower face making the jawline less distinct and giving the appearance of encroaching jowliness. But why passively accept all these changes when you can do something about it? You have much to gain by early maintenance and certain lifestyle changes.

There are three key elements to avoiding this: eating healthily, flushing the system with lots of water, and polishing/massaging the skin's surface. In paintings you can see that the facial skin of affluent Victorian women was much clearer than their poorer counterparts. This porcelain perfection was due to the facial treatments they could afford, which kept their features firmer and younger for longer. This is observable in any culture. Women exposed to the sun, eating a poor diet and with little time to consider their beauty needs show a marked difference in skin quality.

NATURAL OILS

Fruit, plant and nut oils have their uses in your skincare regime. Rich in vitamins and minerals, they can help you maintain healthy skin. Apricot oil nourishes the skin; avocado is a natural sun screen for mildly sunny days; passion flower oil mixed with evening primrose oil increases skin elasticity; peachnut oil is a good choice for facial massage; jojoba oil is good for oily or sensitive skins and olive oil can help to relieve sunburn.

HOW THE SKIN AGES

Your skin isn't just an external covering, like a glove, but an amazing, living breathing organ as essential to your functioning as your heart, liver or lungs. It is the body's largest organ and covers between 15 and 20 square feet. In every square inch there are 15 feet of blood vessels, 12 feet of nerves, 100 sweat glands and over 1500 sensory receptors.

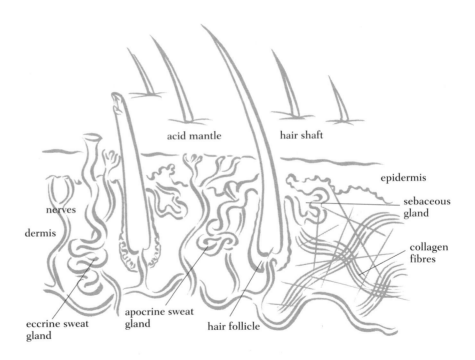

cross section of skin

The skin has two layers. The epidermis is the external layer of skin, a protective barrier to the skin organ beneath. This extremely thin outer layer is composed of dead skin cells, but unfortunately this is the only part of the skin we see and here the sins of unhealthy living are all too visible. The dead skin cells are being shed constantly. When this process slows down – when we age, when our health is poor or when we are eating the wrong diet – the renewal of our cells also slows right down. The deepest portion of the epidermis is the basal layer, which is alive. Its job is to produce these endless layers of cells that gradually move outwards as they mature and form the protective layer of outer dead skin cells. It is this layer that absorbs moisturizers, which are very effective when regularly applied as they plump up the dead cells for up to 12 hours, making the skin appear more youthful and less wrinkled. When you are young these older dead cells are shed naturally, but as you age they tend to accumulate, leading to grey, tired, choked skin. Understanding this is the key to helping your skin stay young and beautiful. Regular exfoliation is vital to slough off this build up, exposing the more supple, youthful and lustrous layer beneath.

The epidermis is connected to the dermis. The dermis rests upon a protective fatty layer, which in turn is built upon a bed of muscle, and it contains a whole network of vital systems: the blood vessels that feed the skin, the nerve system that continually transports sensations to the brain, sweat glands that regulate temperature and oil (or sebaceous) glands that maintain the happy functioning of the skin itself. The substance that contains all these systems is collagen: a strong rubbery protein that plays a major structural role in all mammals.

The state of this collagen is the key to the way that your skin ages. When collagen is young it is like a mesh of well-organized fibres, all sitting neatly and snugly in a tight, regular pattern. As it ages, this order begins to break down and where the collagen is no longer taut wrinkles begin to form. This is why you notice wrinkles appearing first around your mouth. Think of your face like a piece of paper. When you repeatedly smile and speak, the paper is being folded and unfolded over and over again and a crease is soon etched into the formerly smooth surface. Fortunately, unlike a piece of paper, it usually takes more than 20 years for your skin to show these signs of expressive repetition.

Collagen is the key element of the skin's structure, and within it lies another important fibre called elastin. Elastin creates the skin's elasticity. If you think of a pair of leggings, the collagen is like the fabric that forms the structure of the trousers, and the elastin is the Lycra that provides its snug stretch and fit. If you overstretch the Lycra or leave it out in the sun incessantly, your leggings will become less clingy and responsive to your shape and movements. The chemical term for the equivalent structural deterioration in the skin of both collagen and elastin, is oxidation. Once the tone of the collagen and elastin has been lost, wrinkles march relentlessly across the surface of your skin. This process is the result of accumulated exposure to the sun, constant usage, such as smiling or even pulling at the skin with a towel, and decreased blood supply leading to less nutrition reaching the skin.

HORMONAL CHANGES

Oestrogen levels gradually dip as we move through adult life until very small amounts of the female hormone remain at menopause. Not only is falling oestrogen production connected to loss of childbearing ability, the start of hot sweats and an increased chance of heart disease, it also leads to observable changes in skin quality. With less oestrogen, our skin becomes drier, more wrinkled, thinner, older looking and may develop broken capillaries, which look like tiny fine red doodles on your face. Incidentally, the herbal remedy witch hazel is a good choice for broken capillaries.

Don't blame oestrogen withdrawal for all these problems, however. Women who smoke are five times more likely to suffer premature wrinkles than non-smokers, and the extent of their wrinkles is directly connected to the number of cigarettes they smoke. If you are taking HRT you will find that this synthetic hormone will benefit your skin. If you have had a hysterectomy, you will not be at increased risk of uterine cancer and HRT can be a good choice both for its skin-salving qualities and its positive effect on your heart.

CELL REJUVENATION: THE KEY TO YOUTHFUL SKIN

The most important element in sustaining younger looking skin is aiding the skin in its process of dead cell removal. As we age, our skin becomes less efficient at ridding itself of dead skin cells with the result that the epidermis begins to look older, greyer and more wrinkled. Helping to increase the speed of the turnover of these dead skin cells will make vast improvements in your skin. There are a number of different approaches you can take to speed up the process of cell renewal and ensure that your skin is always smooth and glowing.

Regularly rubbing any part of your body can help to slow the visible effects of the passage of time. By stimulating the surface of your skin gently with your fingertips you increase the circulation and speed up the process of cell renewal. You can make small circular massaging movements every day for a few minutes. Your skin will feel warmer and glow as the blood delivery is increased, but avoid the delicate areas around the eyes, which can be over-stretched by too much well-intentioned friction.

Did you know...

Your body needs vitamin D before it can absorb calcium and phosphorus from food. These nutrients are needed for healthy skin and strong bones and teeth. Your body makes vitamin D when it has adequate exposure to the sun; however, if you are indoors most of the time, or wear clothes covering most of your skin, choose foods containing egg yolks, fortified margarine and oily fish to supply this important micronutrient.

Simply

89

Radiant

POLISHING

I am a great believer in body polishing, but do not believe in exfoliation. Body polishing is gentle to the skin, exfoliation can be harsh and scratch the skin. Polishing is completely natural, easy to achieve, and has the power to literally make your skin glow. What's more, it's extremely good for your skin.

Regular polishing with either water or almond oil mixed into a paste with oatmeal helps to prevent skin from building up unwanted thick layers, while also stimulating blood flow to the skin's surface. It will remove the dead cells and nourish the skin, without scratching it. These de-clogging and invigorating benefits help the skin to function properly and even assist the work carried out beneath the surface by the lymphatic, circulatory and nervous systems. These systems perform functions that are crucial to help our skin remain clear, smooth and translucent.

If the surface layer is kept free from unwanted cells its excretory activities can continue unimpeded and you are much less likely to get clogged pores, spots and a dull complexion. Polishing away the dead cells helps prevent these skin nasties occurring, but it has a second, deeper benefit: it also stimulates cell reproduction lower down in the epidermis, meaning you get lots of lovely new skin cells making their way towards the surface.

However, it is important not to be too vigorous in our good intentions. You need to use a cream that includes grains that exfoliate without feeling abrasive. If you are too rough on your skin you can damage the underlying tissue and create darker pigmentation marks and broken capillaries. Always stroke, and never scour, your skin. I recommend polishing the skin gently with a cloth after applying a facial therapy oil twice a day in order to remove dead skin and to boost circulation.

A further polishing option is to use a handful of sea salt (although this is not suitable for dry skin) mixed with a few drops of lavender or tea tree oil which detoxifies and cleanses. Using your chosen preparation once a

Did you know...

Eating wholegrains, nuts and pulses (legumes) will supply the manganese needed for firm skin and strong bones.

week is an ideal way of refining the skin's texture, clearing the pores and improving the skin's circulation. Pay special attention to the head where the routine is: neck, face, ears, back of head. And remember, you need only use a light touch.

FRUIT ACIDS

Until fairly recently, there was little that over-the-counter lotions could really do for your skin. There were all sorts of chemical potions making all manner of promises, but beyond a good moisturizer that would effectively rehydrate your skin for 12 hours at a time, most were a waste of money. None of these non-prescription treatments were actually able to penetrate the dermis and bring about any long-term change.

However, today, the regular use of AHAs (alpha-hydroxy acids), sometimes called fruit acids, can make a difference to the condition of your skin, when combined with the use of moisturizer. Fruit acids are extracted from natural substances such as citrus fruit, grapes, milk and sugar cane. Cleopatra was an early devotee – she used to wash her face in wine. Although you can buy them mixed with moisturizer or sunblock, it is better to use a purer product, either in cream, gel or lotion. AHA-based products do not claim to enter the skin: instead they work specifically on the continually changing layer of dead skin cells that form the epidermis. They exfoliate without effort by dissolving the 'glue' that holds the dead skin cells together. AHAs are an excellent maintenance tool when used in over-the-counter concentrations of less than ten per cent, encouraging the skin to shed excess dead skin cells, which results in smoother, softer, clearer, more wrinkle-free skin. They can even lighten blemishes and repair superficial sun damage. Think of them as a safe refresher for your skin, but bear in mind there is a risk of irritation with sensitive skins and over-use.

Did you know...

Vitamin E is one of the most powerful natural antioxidants. In combination with vitamin C, it blocks the effects of free radicals that damage the skin and joints and break down the immune system.

Good sources of vitamin E include nuts, seeds, oils made from nuts and seeds, and wheatgerm.

91

Simply

Radiant

Don't confuse them with AHA peels, which are much higher doses and actually burn off the top layers of skin: these are not suitable for home treatment in a skin care routine.

Use your chosen fruit acid product at least several times a week for several months. Although you can use them every day, it is better to be more sparing and give your skin a rest period. Because they work by irritating the skin and encouraging a more rapid cell turnover, they can lead to redness and itching. Use them every other night for six months, before taking a month's break. The skin needs a rest period. Older women can use a stronger preparation with more frequency. Nobody knows if fruit acids can actually slow down the deterioration of the skin, but they certainly produce visibly more youthful-looking skin, blemishes fade and the collagen layer feels tighter.

MOISTURIZING FACE MASK

For older skins, I have always recommended polishing with almond oil, but recently I was on a chat-show on Carlton Television called *The A–Z of Food and Beauty* with my friend Peter Vaughan: he recommended a fabulously nourishing face mask. Grate an avocado stone and watch it oxidize from white to red. Add a little yogurt and apply it to your face with your fingers. It makes a beautiful polisher. The avocado is rich in vitamins and oils, and since using this concoction I can really feel the difference in my face.

FACIAL EXERCISES

If you chew your food well, smile don't frown, and use a lot of eye movement rather than living with the mask of a static expression, your face will get all the exercise it needs. I don't believe it's very practical to sit in front of a mirror pulling faces.

GROWTHS

I cannot emphasize enough that if you find any unusual growth upon your skin you should always go to your doctor for his opinion.

MID-LIFE ACNE

What could be more distressing? You made it through the ravages of your hormonal teens, and finally in your twenties and thirties enjoyed blemish-free, spot-free skin – bar a few breakouts tied in to your monthly cycle – and now, as you reach your menopause you've noticed that the cussed blotches of acne are returning.

Mid-life acne is an irritating facet of getting older that is caused by changing hormone levels. In some cases, outbreaks occur after menopause due to levels of the male hormone testosterone rising, while levels of oestrogen fall. But there are two forms of acne, and what you are most likely to suffer in middle age is not Acne Vulgaris, but Acne Rosacea.

Acne Vulgaris is an inflammatory condition of the sebaceous (oil) glands, which is why it occurs most where those glands are most active, such as on the face and back, and during the teenage years when excess oil blocks the pores and hair follicles, and bacterial build-up and infection leads to spots. Never pick a spot. Instead gently stimulate the area around the spot with your fingers. The infection will be brought into the shaft of the spot, and manipulating the skin will encourage blood flow into the damaged follicle, healing it quicker. Beware of overstimulating the follicle, which will result in an overproduction of oil from the sebaceous gland. The follicle will not be able to accommodate the extra oil and will distort or break into the surrounding follicles.

In middle life, you are more likely to experience Acne Rosacea. You might notice that your face is flushed and red, and perhaps has severe

Did you know...

Vitamin C is needed to make collagen, a substance needed for healthy skin, joints, bones and teeth. Blackcurrants, strawberries and potatoes are good sources of vitamin C.

Simply

93

Radiant

dryness and irritation around the nose, cheeks, chin or forehead. When you go out into the cold, or emerge back into the warm, your face seems overly keen to respond with a vivid red hue. This is because the highly sensitive mucous membranes of the throat, nose and sinuses are being stimulated in response to the wrong foods, hay fever, emotional stress or alcohol.

Certain foods seem to aggravate this embarrassing inflammation. If you suffer, look at the following table to see which foods you should avoid and which you should eat more of.

Eat More	Eat Less
fresh fruit (not oranges),	spicy food
fresh vegetables and salad	processed food
wholegrains such as rice	alcohol
and rye (not wheat)	red meat
live yogurt	deep-fried food
garlic	cheese
onions	sugar
seeds and nuts	oranges
fresh fish	cow's milk
	carbonated drinks
	coffee
	wheat-based cereals
	chocolate

Don't forget to drink plenty of water for internal detoxification.

Protect your face from the sun with sun block. Drink eight to ten glasses of water to flush out the facial tissues, and if you do drink alcohol make sure it is with food and water. Cleanse and moisturize with almond oil or a little Vaseline softened in the palm of your hand. Massage your skin delicately with a gentle 'palming' action to calm your irritated nerve endings. This is a light stroking action, using the palms, which corrects imbalances in different parts of the body and is more effective than a deep massage. The palms radiate heat and have a powerful healing action.

SUN DAMAGE

When you were younger your skin had a higher sebum content and a greater moisture level. Each year your drying skin becomes increasingly prone to sun damage. I do not advocate sun-bathing, even with a high factor cream. These protection creams clog your skin. I would not suggest using a cream with a protection factor higher than five to seven. Anything more is potentially damaging, so instead stick to the shade knowing that your chosen moisturizer will protect you and limit the effect of the sun's rays. Your body will absorb the small amount of sunlight it requires to form vitamin D without requiring you to sun worship.

BHARTI'S SKINCARE ROUTINE

A good skin care routine is one that has long-term benefits as well as superficial advantages. It must make sense, and it must work at a deeper level, doing whatever possible to maintain the infrastructure of the skin. It must be a soothing, easily learned and enjoyable process otherwise you simply won't do it! If you follow nothing more than my simple skin care routine, you will have made a great improvement to your image as well as helping your skin to become more healthy. It won't stop the clock, but it can make a definite difference to the face you present to the world each day.

CLEANSING

Cleansing is critical. You need to be able to remove the oily, gritty debris of the modern environment, particularly if you live in a city. I recommend washing your face with water that feels warm to the touch and a mild soap or cleanser that suits you. I'm not against using an unperfumed soft soap, but it can have a drying effect. Get to know your skin: if it looks taut and tight after cleansing, the product you are using is not right for you. You want to avoid drying out the upper layer of your epidermis. Using water that is warmer than blood will encourage your blood vessels to dilate and increase your circulation. It will also be warm enough to dissolve the oils and dirt upon your skin. Avoid using perfumed soaps – they offer no benefits, and may actually irritate your skin. The important thing is to make sure you are using a product that washes off without leaving a residue.

You need to build up a rich lather that will remove make-up, dead cells, excess oils and the dirt of pollution. Leaving any of these substances behind is likely to irritate, and even inflame, your skin. Most people have a combination skin, with areas of oily, dry and normal, but as a general rule the skin dries out as we age. The state of our skin's hydration can also alter from day to day, so the best thing is to ignore what you see and simply take your level of skin cleanliness back to the bottom line with your rich lather each time.

When you have massaged the lather into your skin with your fingertips, not forgetting the sides of your nose, your eyebrows, your neck and your eyelids, for a good 30 seconds, wash it away with copious quantities of clean water that feels warm to the touch. Then repeat the process, but this time follow the warm water rinse with a cold water refresher. This will close any open pores.

Dry your face and enjoy using your towel to polish away any residual dead skin cells that the washing process failed to remove. Towel briskly, but gently, at least once a day, and always from the bottom up – you want to avoid introducing your skin to gravity.

MOISTURIZING

Unfortunately, it is impossible for a skin cleanser or soap to distinguish between your own natural skin oils, with their healthy moisturizing abilities, and the oily debris of environmental pollution. So once you've washed your face you do need to remoisturize.

In general, women with oily skin should bypass heavy, oil-based creams; if you have dry skin you should avoid harsh astringents, but use moisturizer to prevent moisture loss. For normal and combination skins don't use anything that is too harsh or overstimulating.

My recommendation for a good moisturizer is simply that you do not over-moisturize the skin. Let your skin work for itself. If you put too much fabric softener on clothes it makes them limp, not fluffy. Don't take away the skin's ability to moisturize itself, using a smaller amount of moisturizer will encourage the sebum in your skin to self-regulate. You can consider using a moisturizer that contains an AHA, but this should only be used once a day, preferably in the morning. You should also use a sunscreen every day to protect your skin from the sun's rays (yes, even on a drab winter day the damage is cumulative). Use a moisturizer that contains a sun screen of at least factor ten for your face.

Moisturizers are very beneficial, but they are very simple in the way they work and do not last longer than 12 hours. They are certainly not a treatment, because they produce no permanent change, but in a purely cosmetic way they make a good deal of difference. For the time they are effective they will trap moisture in the layer of dead skin cells that cover the surface of your skin, helping you to look and feel better and younger. The condition of this layer can vary from dry to scaly, to smooth and lustrous, simply by virtue of the amount of moisturizer temporarily trapped in it. By applying moisturizer you are mimicking the effects of the body's oils, which also trap moisture. Unfortunately your own naturally moisturizing oils need to be regularly washed away as they also trap all that horrible pollution and grime.

The way you apply your moisturizer, and other skin treatments, can have benefits. Since ancient times the hands have been used for healing and I'm a great endorser of using these marvellous extremities. Gentle massage stimulates nerve endings in the skin that are connected to our vital organs. As products are applied using various routines, such as palming, toxins are gradually removed, tension drains away and the skin's balance is restored. There are no miracle cures, so you need to apply these techniques consistently and regularly when you have the time to reap the benefits.

A YOUNG SKIN FOR LIFE

Unfortunately, wrinkles last forever, so prevention is far more effective than cure. It really is never too soon, or too late, to adopt certain habits and routines which will slow down the process of deterioration in your skin.

Unfortunately, the current approach to skincare is too cosmetic. Too many beauty houses promote different products for the same job and give

Young looking skin requires a healthy

conflicting advice. In my opinion, the secrets of good skin are simplicity and sympathy. So many of my clients come to me with puffy eyes and unbalanced skin with clogged pores. I believe this is because their skin is either overtreated or wrongly treated. No-one needs to use more than four different skincare products each day, and everyone should have a monthly professional facial that works at a deep level. What every woman also needs is a skincare routine that really works.

But whatever you do to the exterior of your body, never forget the importance of a healthy diet. The skin will deteriorate if the body is poorly nourished and lacking in vitamins, minerals, amino-acids, enzymes and hormones. Beauty really does begin on the inside.

diet and a strict skincare routine

Good sex helps to sustain the bond

Maturing Sexuality

Your sexual relationship is, potentially, a wonderfully intimate way of deepening the love you share with your partner as you age, connecting you both physically and mentally. Loving each other leads to better love making, and having good sex will sustain your love. Thankfully this is becoming much easier now we are moving out of the era in which women cease to view themselves as sexual creatures on reaching menopause. Passing the big Four-O no longer leads to a set of social and sexual barriers. No longer do we face a future where we become insignificant on reaching 40 and believe we have to stop having sex just because we've been through menopause.

There is a common myth that menopause marks the beginning of a woman's sexual decline, but fortunately we have moved on from the era when our only purpose in life was youthfulness and an ability to reproduce, adorn and be somebody's other half, and when all that was no longer an option we were forced to adopt sensual purdah – wearing drab clothes and taking up knitting, macrame and dog walking. Now we can dye our hair, wear brightly coloured clothes, go dancing, embark on a new career, relish our freedom and independence, and expect to have sex for as long as we wish – into our seventies and beyond. Many women continue to have healthy, loving sex lives long after menopause, for we are no longer under any pressure to view ourselves as having a sell-by date. Think Jane Fonda, Sophia Loren, Raquel Welch, Joan Collins: all have loving partners and are perfect examples of the seven out of ten women who still enjoy active sex lives after menopause, recognizing that mature love-making is a health-enhancing activity that provides life with an edge and sparkle.

We can still have orgasms: our desire and enjoyment of sensual and sexual love, which I believe is a fundamental component of marriage, is not lost. A recent survey showed that all those who were interested in sex before menopause said they were still interested afterwards. Another survey showed that many women found their sex drive was either unchanged, or had actually *increased* after menopause. If we have divorced or lost a partner and feel able emotionally to move on, we can start a new relationship at any time in our lives. The years during and after your menopause can be some of the most exciting, challenging, dynamic and physically satisfying. There can be a general slowing down, a more considered approach to sex, with an emphasis on the comfort and intimacy of a loving relationship and less focus on orgasm.

Another good reason not to stop having sex is that it is really good for you. According to research conducted by the Athena Institute for Women's Wellness Research in America, women who are approaching menopause and still having sex weekly, experience fewer hot sweats than those who are not sexually active. There is no reason why a woman should ever lose her sense of femininity, or cease being attractive to the right person, despite getting older.

But many women find that because of falling oestrogen levels, sex feels different after menopause – and this is quite normal. One woman in

Regular love-making will enable you

every five loses her sex drive altogether, one in five suffers vaginal dryness, one in six finds it difficult to reach orgasm and one in 12 suffers from painful intercourse. However much you want to have a loving sex life, such changes can lead to both physical and psychological effects. But there are holistic solutions that should put your sexual life back on track. You are more likely to still enjoy an active sex life after menopause if you had a rewarding sexual relationship before it, physical and emotional fitness, an acceptance of your body, and a positive attitude towards maturing and sex. Regular love-making or masturbation will enable you to continue being sexually active as you grow older by keeping your genitals healthy and helping to keep up your levels of vaginal lubrication.

Men in particular are driven by their hormones to need sex throughout their lives, so if you retreat from sex at menopause this can lead to relationship difficulties, and ultimately depression. If you are feeling depressed it is very important to see your doctor. And don't worry: she will have heard countless tales like yours. The support of your partner is very important at this time in your life so ask if he will accompany you, and hopefully your doctor will be able to ease the problem before it gets any worse.

LIBIDO

Some women find that they feel less interested in sex after menopause. Your libido is controlled by a complex cocktail of sex hormones, including oestrogen and progesterone and the male hormone, testosterone. All women make small amounts of male hormone in their ovaries and this hormone is the key to sex drive. When the ovaries no longer function, after menopause, levels of the hormone drop. But it's not all bad news.

to continue to be active as you mature

Did you know...

Fatigue and depression may be due to low levels of B vitamins in the diet. Preparing meals based on life-bearing foods supplies the nervous system with these necessary nutrients.

When the ovaries no longer make enough, the production of sex drive hormones is taken over in other parts of the body including the adrenal glands, skin, pineal gland and body fat stores. Your body can be so successful at this that your sex drive may actually increase without oestrogen to counter-balance them. The downside is the unwanted hairs that also accompany this change in your body's chemistry, but given the efficacy of depilatory creams it seems like a small price to pay.

However, if you have been under a lot of stress your body may not be able to produce sex drive hormones so efficiently. If your libido seems adversely affected, the best treatment is a plant-based diet, vitamin E, magnesium and vitamin B supplements, perhaps with the addition of natural progesterone, which your doctor can prescribe for you.

And remember, it's perfectly normal to experience hormonal dry patches in a marriage. The important element is whether you are both happy with less sexual intimacy, and if you are not, whether you are committed to rediscovering a sexual bond as a top priority. When people ask, 'how do I put the spark back into my love life?' they really mean, 'how do I increase my sexual desire?'

There is some evidence that sexual *drive* declines in both men and women due to natural hormone changes as we age. However, there is no evidence that there is a decline in sexual *desire* as we age. Sex drive is controlled by hormones and external events in life. In women, pregnancy, childbirth and menopause alter levels of hormones and affect sex drive. If you have lost your sex drive (you never seem to want to make love even though you love your partner) and your environment has not changed (you are not on hormonal medication, for example) there may be a biological basis and a healthcare professional may be able to help.

But sexual desire comes from our minds: it is a combination of mood, self-consciousness and relationship. Your loss of desire may not be due to your menopause. You cannot feel like making love if there are problems in your relationship; you are stressed and too tied up with work, running the home or caring for relatives; you feel a lack of sexual confidence or are suffering a mild depression. If you still enjoy cuddling your partner, your lack of desire is unlikely to be due to a lack of love. It may be connected to your changing hormone levels, tiredness, stress, illness or concern about your changing body image.

Unfortunately, if you have poor body image you may feel less desire, however much you wish to create intimacy with your partner. Arousal begins in the mind and if you are clogged with feelings of uncertainty or anxiety it can be difficult to feel in the mood. But do bear in mind that some drugs used for treating certain conditions, such as high blood pressure, can affect your libido, as can feelings of depression. Discuss your concerns with your doctor before they start adding to the problem. You may be given a test for diabetes or thyroid disease, both of which can influence your libido.

If you seem to have a loss of desire, take time to pamper yourself and remind yourself that you are a sensual creature. Create a beautiful setting for intimacy – light candles, buy special bed linen, play music, give yourself a manicure and pedicure, think about your best qualities, do your hair and wear clothes that make you feel attractive. These simple acts of self care can really boost your sexual desire because they feed your feelings of sensuality. They will also help to alleviate any stress you are feeling. Being stressed affects libido so you do need to find time for rest … and exercise. When you exercise you boost your metabolic rate, which burns off excess stress hormones and helps you feel more fully rested.

Also, you should try to get enough sleep – tiredness will really lower your libido. If you smoke, try to stop. Cigarettes really ought to carry the following Government Health Warning: Smoking can kill your sex drive! Don't drink to excess – 21 units is the safe maximum for women a week – any more and you may lower your sex drive and reduce vaginal lubrication.

Take zinc, which will help maintain your sex drive, and evening primrose oil capsules, which contain the essential fatty acids your sex hormones need.

The herbal remedy sarsaparilla helps to overcome a reduced sex drive in women going through menopause. It contains substances that boost the action of the male sex hormones that control libido in women, but avoid taking it if you suffer from excessive facial hair as it can also boost hair growth. Alternatively, try the following homoeopathic remedies: sepia 30C is particularly good if loss of interest is severe and linked with exhaustion; agnus castus 30C if you also have reduced energy levels.

The good news is that your interest in sex is likely to return naturally. Most women start to feel much better as their body adjusts to lower levels of oestrogen. But even if you are already in some sexual difficulty, the good news is that oestrogen creams can reverse the damage in only a few weeks.

PHYSICAL CHANGES

It is common to find that after menopause and a decrease in oestrogen you notice some physical changes that can make sex feel less comfortable, even painful. Your vagina is likely to feel drier, unless you are taking HRT, which helps you remain lubricated, and this can lead to pain during intercourse, so it's a good idea to keep a tube of water-based lubricant discreetly by your bed and slip a little on your finger when you need it. Because the vagina shrinks and its lining becomes thinner, sometimes penetration can be painful or even cause bleeding. If you still feel uncomfortable consider using HRT or perhaps an oestrogen cream, which your doctor can prescribe.

Oestrogen cream is also useful if you have pain in your clitoris. The hood of the clitoris can shrink, exposing the more delicate tissue beneath. Please do confide in your doctor. It should be quite easily cured with either oestrogen tablets or cream, which can also help those women, one in six, who find it increasingly difficult to reach orgasm around the time of menopause due to the decrease in sensitivity of the clitoris as oestrogen levels fall.

Another change that is quite common, yet rarely understood, is that falling oestrogen levels lead your skin to feel less sensitive, and this can interfere with your enjoyment of sex. Start taking evening primrose oil capsules and eat a diet rich in plant hormones, such as broccoli, celery, rhubarb, fennel, green and yellow vegetables and soya beans, if this is troubling you. Ask your partner to give you a sensual massage using 15 drops of aromatherapy oil together with 30 drops of sweet almond oil.

Clary sage is a good oil to use – an antidepressant that can help to alleviate oestrogen-withdrawal symptoms including vaginal dryness. Other good choices are geranium, hyacinth or lavender, which all have similar properties. And neroli, in addition to being an antidepressant and relieving vaginal dryness, is also thought to have sensual properties that can help improve your level of sexual desire. If you would like a homoeopathic aid, then try bryonia 6C, especially if you are also feeling sore and uncomfortable. If you suffer both vaginal dryness and hot sweats, the best choice is lycopodium 30C.

Sometimes difficulties in a sexual relationship can be ascribed to the woman's menopause when they are actually symptoms of a man's ill health. Try to talk to your partner sympathetically if he seems less interested in sex, and don't assume that the problem is being caused by a change in his level of attraction to you. There can be a number of reasons for his change in sexual appetite. If he has problems with his heart he may be anxious about sex. Diabetes can lead to impotence. If he is taking prescription drugs for high blood pressure or diabetes this can affect his libido. Visiting a doctor together can put these concerns into perspective.

107

Simply

Radiant

Did you know...

Slow-release carbohydrates help calm the mind and maintain a healthy and constant level of energy. Make sure your daily diet includes some of the following: rice, beans, lentils, potatoes and wholegrain foods.

CREATING MATURE INTIMACY IN SEX

Did you know...

In addition to maintaining healthy bones and teeth, calcium is needed for normal blood clotting, muscle activity, and function of the nerves.

108

As we age we look for more meaning in life. As you grow older it is no longer enough, if ever it was, to make love with your body. You expect more from sex. You want to make love with your mind, body, heart and soul. However much you might want to show all these things, you might find them difficult to express sexually. You want to build a bridge between what you feel for your partner, and a physical expression of that love. But evolving and maintaining this emotion in motion, year after year, can be a challenge. It can be particularly difficult when our bodies are changing, leading us to feel less confident and therefore less sexual about ourselves. There is a temptation to pine for the younger, more physically confident self, leading sex to become filled with fear, low self esteem, even regret or boredom. But it need not be like this.

In the West there is too much emphasis on sexual performance, and not enough on loving intimacy. The joyful thing is that as you age you know yourself and your partner better, you have wisdom, confidence, self-knowledge and an evolved personality. This is a time when you and your partner can enjoy making love with your minds, as much as your bodies. It is a time when you can start to worry less about sexual performance and more about fostering loving intimacy. The hormonal charge that couples feel when they are first going out together is unlikely to be the template for sex throughout their lives. This is unrealistic. People change and grow, and so does their physical language. Fortunately this change can bring a couple closer together, if they are committed to investing in building intimacy.

THE EVOLUTION OF LOVE

Commitment is the cornerstone of lasting love. Physical closeness and shared trust lead to emotional intimacy, which deepens your physical intimacy. A large component of making a commitment to each other is committing to change. Rather than expecting to stay the same, we are always changing, growing older and wiser, and evolving from our experiences. Consequently our relationships must change along with us. To sustain the richness of sex you and your partner need to acknowledge the evolution of yourselves and your partnership. And at no time does your relationship change as much as mid-life: children are leaving home, you are undergoing physical and hormonal changes, you may be thinking about retirement. Sex may seem rather low on the agenda. If so, you need to take the emphasis off sex for a while and concentrate on fostering intimacy. Here are a number of intimate activities that may help re-focus your attention on each other:

CREATING THE MOOD

Some of my clients complain to me that they feel tired and stressed in the evenings, and sex seems like the last thing on their minds. My advice to them is to have a relaxing hot bath, wash your private parts – remembering that there is nothing wrong in touching yourself – and seduce your husband. When you have good sex it really eases all your stresses. If you don't feel comfortable, or in the mood, for sexual seduction, consider giving your husband a sensate focus massage instead (*see page 110*).

THE IMPORTANCE OF TOUCH

How our body feels to us is much more important than how it looks or what it does. The key to knowing how our body feels is the simple joy of giving and receiving touch. It is the medium through which we communicate on a non-verbal level while making love. Touch has been shown to be vital for newborns of all species to thrive, and skin-to-skin contact affects our health throughout all stages of our lives. When you are married, or in a long-term relationship, you are reliant on your partner, and they on you, for the majority of touches external to themselves. After you and your partner have been together for many years, you have probably fallen into familiar patterns of touching. You have a well-rehearsed vocabulary of sexual and non-sexual touch. Perhaps one always holds the other in bed. Maybe one of you always stands on tiptoes while you are hugging. Do you always wrap your arms around each other the same way when you hug? Try the sensate focus massage for a fresh and invigorating new perspective.

I am a great advocate of sensual touching. A healthy, loving sex life does not always have to involve sex. There should never be pressure to have sex. When two people love each other and are comfortable expressing affection through hugging and touching each other's bodies sex will be much easier. Stroking each other's skin in a non-sexual way is a natural therapy. If you massage and soothe each other's tired limbs you will maintain a precious familiarity with each other's bodies. This will make sex much more relaxed, while nourishing your relationship with the mental intimacy that it creates. Lie your partner on his front, and sit naked upon his buttocks before you begin to massage him. Clients to whom I have recommended this approach say that it has completely changed their life and their husbands are very quickly aroused by this approach.

SENSATE FOCUS MASSAGE

The pioneering sex researchers, Masters and Johnson, evolved a form of treatment for couples who are feeling disinterested in sex, which is often encouraged by sex therapists today. Sensate focus describes a way of touching in which you focus your attention as closely as possible upon the sensations in your skin at the point where your fingers meet your partner. Try not to think about where to touch next, just lose yourself in the moment. Penetrative sex is banned, instead take turns to explore each other for up to half an hour each, avoiding erogenous zones such as the breasts and genitals.

The sensate focus touch is a caress. A delicate but definite touch that is not a massage, rub, pressure stroke or brushing glide. Instead it is very slow – make your fingers travel at half the speed they would normally when stroking your partner. It is focused – think about the temperature and texture of what you are touching. It is now – don't think about past or future. It is sensual, not sexual – as you touch your partner focus on the pleasure of their skin contact and the intimacy that such a touch creates, but remember your touch carries no implicit pressure to have sex.

It is a way to escape the tension of performance pressure. Worrying 'am I doing this right' or 'does he like this' is inhibiting. It keeps us separate from our partners and can drown out sexual arousal. Focusing instead on the touch, and switching roles so you both explore each other in this way removes the pressure to perform. It also allows you to express your love both non-verbally and non-sexually to your partner. Swapping touches also allows you to break out of the familiar roles in which a couple cast themselves after a number of years together. Is your partner the one who always initiates sex? Do you touch more than him? Does touching always lead to sex? Sensate focus touches allow you to step outside your usual roles and become both passive and active. Equality is very important in a healthy loving relationship.

Once you are both comfortable with the sensate focus massage, try moving on to genital sensate focusing in which you can touch your erotic areas.

THE FACE TOUCH

This is a touching massage that can create as much emotional closeness as sexual bonding. If you feel sexually in a rut, or feel pressure always to have sex, this massage can make a very energizing change. One partner sits with their back against a sofa, wall or headboard, with a pillow or cushion in their lap. The passive partner lies back, still clothed, with their head in the centre of the cushion. Take a small amount of oil or lotion and caress your lover's face, keeping your touch light, sensuous and slow. Move your fingers over his forehead, down his cheeks, around his nose, across the delicate under-eye area and around the ears. Do this for 15 minutes and then change places. This is a massage of discovery. As we age, both men and women deeply appreciate being really treasured and explored in this way. But neither of you need speak, or remove your clothes, to fully experience the value of this sensually enriching technique.

CO-BREATHING

Parents show their love for their baby by spending time cuddling and holding their child. This nurturing intimacy increases a child's self esteem and leads it to feel safe, secure, loved and whole. We can offer the same gift to our partner. Instead of saying 'I love you', try to put some extra meat of experience on the dry bones of those oft-repeated words. Hold, stroke and physically calm your partner in a non-sexual, non-verbal manner that will help you recreate, or reaffirm, your intimate connection. Try this if you are wound up after work, in the mornings before you get up or just before you fall asleep.

Light a candle, and lie together in bed facing the same direction and snuggled up in a 'spoons' embrace where one person's back is nuzzled into the other person's front and their arm is draped tenderly around the waist

Non-sexual touching will help you

of the person in front. Lie still, let go of tension and rather than talking become aware of each other's breathing. Decrease your breathing rate by taking several deep breaths together, and exhaling. Imagine that you are both sinking down deeper into the bed, you are together, and you both feel warm and inseparable. After a few minutes, you may become aware that you are breathing at the same rate as each other.

LOOK INTO MY SOUL

The key element that allows onlookers to discern whether a couple love each other or just like each other is the amount of time the couple spend looking into each other's eyes. Even if this is something you haven't done very much since you were courting, you can recreate the intense feelings of intimacy it offers at any point in your relationship together. In mid-life it is particularly valuable because you feel you are looking deep into the soul of the person you have chosen to share your life with, part way along that journey.

Lie on your bed, or sit facing each other. Hold hands and gaze into each other's eyes for a few minutes. Don't talk. Enjoy the feelings of intensity that arise through this process of reconnection. This is a way of being with each other, rather than talking at each other or co-existing alongside each other. If you do this together from time to time you will be able to gauge different reactions at different times and develop your non-verbal language of the soul.

Did you know...

Phosphorus, found in rich supply in life-bearing foods, works with calcium to build strong bones and teeth.

113

Simply

Radiant

to reaffirm your intimate connection

MASSAGE AND

Acupressure

Acupressure uses fingertips to effect

If you can learn to use your own hands as a curative tool you will have knowledge about yourself you are unlikely ever to forget. Using manual movements upon different parts of your body can be extremely beneficial as a way of accessing inner radiance, and easing some of the symptoms of menopause. The application may be via your skin, using the hands as a curative pressure therapy tool, but the effect is upon your inner body. Acupressure is the application of deep fingertip or thumb pressure at specific points on the body. Stimulating the nerve endings can bring a change in your health. It is an ancient Oriental system of treatment which is easy to learn, free from side effects and takes only a short time to apply. It can be used to promote general health and wellbeing as well as relieving a wide range of common ailments. It draws on the same principles as acupuncture, and, as a qualified acupuncturist, I am a great exponent of these simple deep-focus massages. They are accessible, easy to apply and very practical in their benefits.

Did you know...

Beans, lentils, nuts, seeds and all the other life-bearing foods are rich in B-complex vitamins, and therefore very beneficial for your nervous system. They have a calming and stabilizing effect.

pressure on specific points of the body

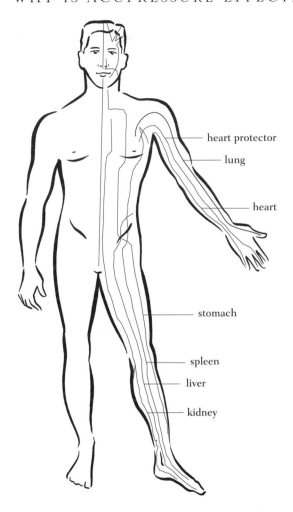

heart protector

lung

heart

stomach

spleen

liver

kidney

meridians

The ancient Chinese believed that energy circulated in the body along specific pathways, which they called meridians, and in a particular direction. They believed that the balance of energy from top to bottom, side to side, and from inside to outside the body was of great importance. This harmony and balance makes up the essence of the philosophy of yin and yang: that everything has an equal and opposite. The balance between these opposites is never static, but is always dynamic, constantly fluctuating and changing. But the Chinese believed that when a person became too unbalanced, they would need treatment to reset and restore their inner harmony, for without it, this disharmony would result in all manner of physical and emotional problems requiring correction. Early acupuncturists developed a sophisticated system of laws, from which followed a set of ground rules about how to treat an ailing patient. The good thing is that you don't need to understand this system to benefit from acupuncture and its little sister, acupressure. Modern-day researchers have found that the application of the technique does work in a highly significant proportion of patients, which explains why it has been adopted so readily despite its complex theory.

The Chinese believed that as well as being in balance, the essential energy (called chi) had to be able to circulate freely around the meridians. If there was a break in its easy movement anywhere, then an illness would result. The way to remedy this is to insert a needle at the point of discomfort, or in the case of acupressure to give a deep point massage to the same blockage.

Did you know...

The slow, steady flow of energy from the digestion of grains, pulses (legumes) and other starchy foods has a calming effect on the brain, and provides a constant source of fuel for active muscles.

Simply

119

Radiant

WHY DOES IT WORK?

You may find the Chinese belief in energy circulation difficult to grasp, but there are two other, more scientific explanations for why acupuncture and acupressure are so effective. Firstly, as the bundles of nerve fibres running through our bodies contain two sorts of nerve: touch and pain, by stimulating the touch nerves with a needle or deep massage, the pain fibres transmit less messages to the nerve receptors in the brain. Secondly, it is possible that needling or massaging the energy points causes the body to release a dose of its own natural painkillers, called endorphins.

THE METHOD

If you are treating a persistent problem that has lasted longer than two weeks, you may need to apply acupressure for at least 20 treatments (two to three times a week). If your problem is more recent, you may need just a few treatments over the course of a couple of days. Sometimes, with a minor ailment, a single session can bring relief.

Treat each point for two to three minutes, or until you feel a deep, achy, numb feeling in the point you are working on. Always work your fingers deeply over the specified point to locate the most tender area, and concentrate on this. If acupressure is not uncomfortable to begin with, then increase the pressure. A small amount of pain is actually curative, and any discomfort will soon pass. When you use a moisturizer, as with all body lotions, you want all evidence of the cream to disappear, so don't use so much that you are left with a greasy oil slick. Use only the amount that disappears readily into the skin.

BHARTI'S FOUR MASSAGE TECHNIQUES

There are four main techniques I encourage you to learn in order to give effective self-massage, and massage to your partner. You can use each of them to varying degrees to add some variety to your massage regimen, but if your skin is intact and you are not over-sensitive, it is better to use the deepest massage you can.

PINCHING

(For the face and body). Use tiny pinches with the thumb and index fingers in small areas like the temple. For larger areas such as the shoulder, pinch with the thumb and four fingers. Pinching is a fast action which activates the skin's nerve endings and revives the cells, helping to drain away waste via the lymph. It is a deeper technique.

PALMING

(For the face and body). A light, stroking action with the palms corrects imbalances in different parts of the body and can be more effective than a deep massage. The palms radiate heat and have a powerful, magnetic healing action.

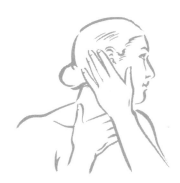

FINGER BALLS

(For the face, scalp and body). Using a series of small, circular movements you stimulate the nerve endings and activate blood vessels and the lymphatic system. The balls of your fingers are highly sensitive.

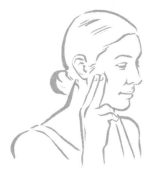

FEATHER MASSAGE

(For the face and body). Use the fingers to create light, feathery upward strokes to stimulate the para-sympathetic nervous system. This is particularly suitable for those with a low pain threshold, very sensitive skin or for using upon parts of the body that are swollen.

THE TOP PRESSURE POINTS FOR
REJUVENATION

TAIYANG

Relaxes tense facial muscles, revitalizes expression and smooths complexion.

Location: one thumb width beyond the eyebrow, in a dip in the skin halfway between the outer edge of the eyebrow and the corner of the eye. Apply circular pressure using your index finger for about a minute.

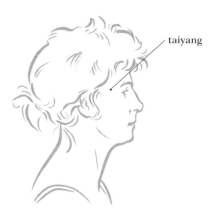

taiyang

Did you know...

Normal cell development is vital for a long and beautiful life. Molybdenum, a mineral found in pulses (legumes), wholegrains and leafy vegetables, is needed for healthy genetic activity in tissues.

SPLEEN 6

Increases sexual vitality, limits water retention and balances hormonal activity.

Location: four finger widths above the tip of the prominent bone on the inside of the ankle, just behind the shin bone. Measure with one hand and apply pressure with the middle or index finger of the other. This is where the spleen, liver and kidney meridians meet. A very powerful acupressure point.

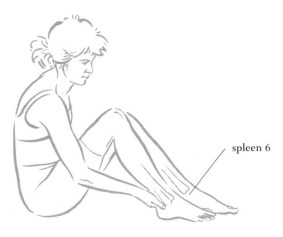

spleen 6

HEART 7

Calms the nervous system and relieves mental tension, anxiety and sleeplessness.

Location: Draw an imaginary straight line on the palm, starting at the web of the third finger and little finger, and finishing at the wrist. It lies at the junction of this line and the wrist crease. Support the wrist with the fingers of the opposite hand, with the palm facing upwards, then locate the point with the thumb. Use your thumb to apply pressure with a pumping action for approximately a minute.

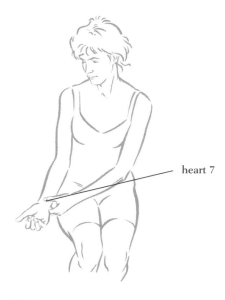

heart 7

URINARY BLADDER 60

Boosts immune system and urinary system, increases mobility and relieves aches, pains and swelling in the legs and feet.

Location: In the hollow between the ankle bone and the Achilles tendon, on the outer side of the foot. Wrap the index finger around the ankle and apply pressure with the thumb. Avoid during pregnancy.

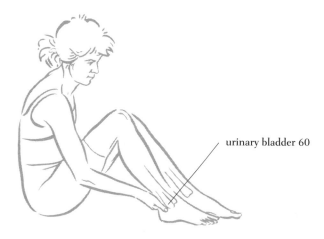

urinary bladder 60

LIVER 3

Improves liver function and boosts the immune system, cuts stress, regulates blood pressure, reduces irritability, combats depression, improves circulation in the legs, relieves cramp and helps prevent varicose veins.

Location: On the upper surface of the foot, approximately two thumb-widths below the web between the big toe and the second toe. Place your fingers under your feet and use your thumb to apply pressure in the hollow between the bones.

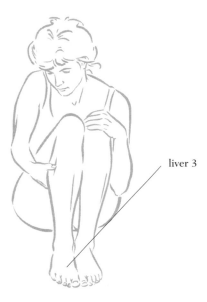

liver 3

GOVERNING VESSEL 14

A good preventative cure-all.

Location: When the head is bent forwards, two vertebrae stand out prominently where the top of the spine meets the base of the neck. The point is located in between the two vertebrae. Reach over your shoulder with one hand and apply firm pressure with the tip of your first or second finger, with your neck in an upright position.

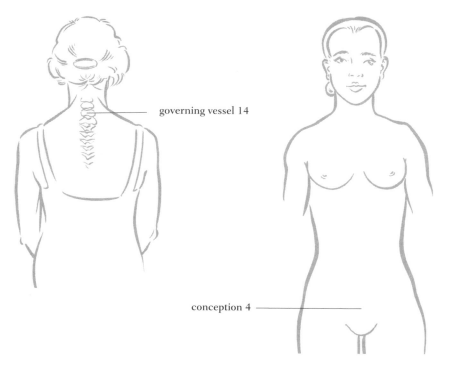

governing vessel 14

conception 4

PRESSURE POINTS FOR ENHANCING SEXUALITY

Oriental medicine considers sex a vital element of the human life-force. Sexual energy is thought to invigorate all the organs of the body, including the brain, while weakened sexual vitality can lead to various problems. You can improve your sexual health by exercising regularly, sleeping long enough, limiting stress and eating a healthy diet. To build sexual vitality you might also consider working on the following acupressure points.

CONCEPTION VESSEL 4 (above)
Increases sexual potency and vitality, and tones the gynaecological organs.

Location: Measure four finger widths below the navel, and with the middle finger of the other hand apply pressure gently.

CONCEPTION VESSEL

Increases energy levels and sexual vitality.

Location: Two finger widths below the navel. Use gentle rotating movements with the fingertip.

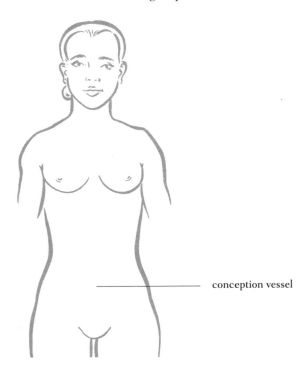

conception vessel

URINARY BLADDER 23

Strengthens the kidneys, which are traditionally related to sexual vitality.

Location: On the lower back, two finger widths on either side of the spine, approximately level with the waist. Push your thumbs into the points.

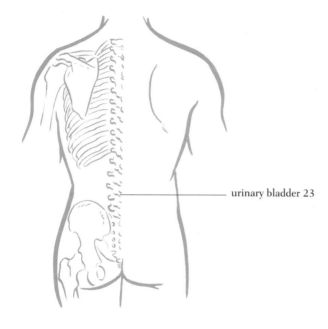

urinary bladder 23

KIDNEY 3

Helps to reinvigorate your interest in sex if you are feeling disinclined.

Location: On the inside of the ankle in the depression just above the ankle bone. Apply pressure with your thumb, pushing slightly downwards towards the heel.

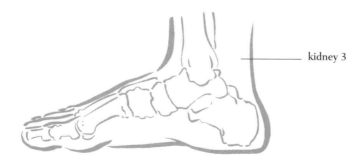

kidney 3

MASSAGE WITH A PARTNER FOR ENHANCING SENSUALITY

This is a very intimate and therapeutic 10-minute massage that has the power to change the energy between you. It can be used as part of foreplay, or simply to create a stronger emotional connection between you.

1   Have a bath together, or bathe independently if you prefer. While your partner is still in the water begin massaging the top of his spine at the base of his neck, using the finger ball method.

2   Dry each other and sit upon the bed. Continue to work up and down his spine, varying the pressure between feathering, pinching and finger balls. It is a good idea to use a body lotion, or a dilute aromatherapy oil. Gradually he will relax and will want to lie down.

3   Encourage him to lie unclothed upon his tummy on the bed. Straddle his buttocks so that your genitals are touching his bottom, reminding him of the warmth and pleasure of your body. Place your hands upon the fleshy part of his buttocks. This is an important gall bladder pressure point. Invigorate the area by pressing firmly upon the buttock and pushing up towards his spine. Repeat this many times, using a deep pressure. This acts like a blood pump, and will invigorate the circulation and increase sexual vitality.

4   Using your fingers as a finger ball, place each hand two inches either side of the vertebrae. Use your knuckles to penetrate into the connective tissue and roll them around, using quite a lot of pressure, which is very soothing.

5   Alternate finger balls with the sensuality of palming, stroking his body before working more deeply upon the areas you have prepared.

Use the palms of your hands to gently stroke your partner, particularly on the inside of his thighs and the soles of his feet.

6   To close the massage, place the flat of your palm at the top of his spine and pass it very lightly down the full length. Do this ten times to soothe your partner who may now be feeling very sensual.

NB. When giving partner-massage to enhance sexuality, it is important to make a strong statement that the massage is not one-sided. Once you have shown him the method, my advice is to encourage your partner to massage you first. After making love, when he is falling asleep, you can then massage him. Being a woman, you will be left with a lot more energy.

A DIY HAND MASSAGE TO EASE HOT SWEATS

Hot sweats are due to hormonal imbalance. They are particularly troublesome to treat, and acupressure offers a safe and often effective way of coping with them. Follow my self treatment acupressure massage, and use it on a regular basis even if you are not actually experiencing a hot sweat at the time of treatment.

This massage works by calming the nervous system, treating the hormonal system, relieving mental tension, anxiety and sleeplessness. It eases breathing difficulties triggered by the anxiety of hot sweats, as well as improving the condition of hands and nails.

1   This fleshy part of the hand is very important, but often overlooked. It benefits the whole upper body, in particular it helps tone the skin and improve the complexion, and it is a good general tonic point that promotes circulation and vital energy. It aids large intestine function and can help relieve constipation. Think of it like a pump that helps to activate the circulation.

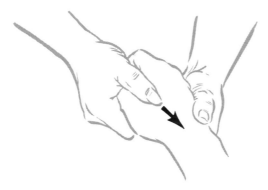

2   Using a firm rocking pressure, move your thumb up the inside of the wrist.

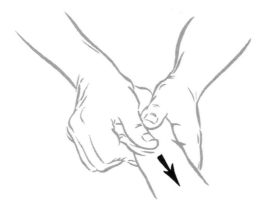

3   Apply pressure to this point, two finger widths from the wrist crease in the depression behind the bone, and angle the pressure slightly down towards the wrist and thumb. Apply sustained pressure and finger balls for a minute to strengthen the respiratory system.

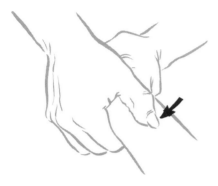

4   Apply finger balls to the middle of the palm between the bones leading to the index and middle fingers, apply pressure angled slightly towards the middle fingers to calm the mind and reduce mental irritation.

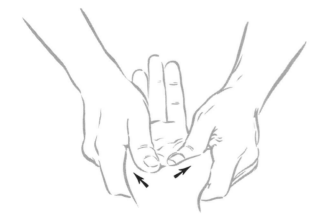

5   In the middle of the wrist crease, apply pressure angling your touch towards the palm of the hand. Press in between the blood vessels and tendons, not directly upon them to promote circulation and relieve faintness.

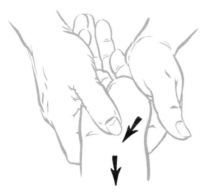

6   Move the thumb three finger widths from the wrist crease. Applying finger balls will calm the mind and relieve anxiety.

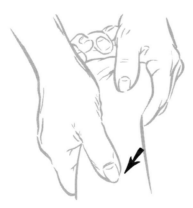

7 Apply pressure to these three points located along the crease line of your wrist to improve circulation, ease breathing, strengthen heart function, calm the mind, and help you sleep.

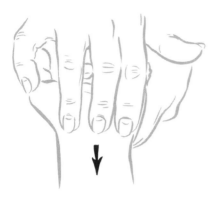

8 Move your fingers three finger widths further up the arm from the wrist crease closest to the palm. Apply gentle pressure angled slightly downwards for 30 seconds to a minute. This stimulates and regulates heart function, and promotes good circulation of blood and energy.

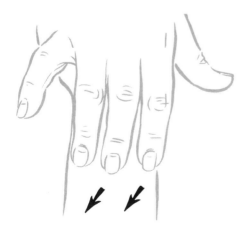

EAR MASSAGE FOR ALL-OVER VITALITY
AND RADIANCE

The relationship between the ear and internal organs was first recorded more than 2,000 years ago. Massaging your ear has enormous benefits. Giving yourself an auricular massage improves the vitality of the whole body, particularly when you are menopausal.

First, remove your earrings. Let your ear guide you to the treatment you require. Press quite hard, and where you have a weakness you will find that your ear hurts at the corresponding point. Do not avoid the area: let the tenderness be your guide to what area of your body needs attention, this applies to all areas treated with acupressure. For an effective, holistic treatment of the entire body follow these simple massage instructions:

1   Stimulating the top of the ear helps with weakness of the diaphragm and the groove here is good for lowering blood pressure.

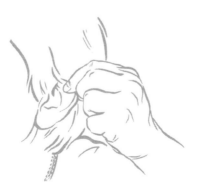

2   (**top of page 137**) Work your way around the ear, making a sequence of deep pinches, and rolling the cartilage between your thumb and forefinger.

3   When we are menopausal one of the target areas that slows down is the liver. Pulling the flange of the ear stimulates the meridian point that corresponds to the liver. Manipulate it with the finger ball method.

4   Pressing on the node in front of the ear, stimulates the lungs and heart, helping to oxygenate the body and improving circulation.

5   Press with a firm pressure in the middle of the ear, against the cartilage.
    This stimulates the adrenal gland which has a strong influence over the
    body's hormonal system.

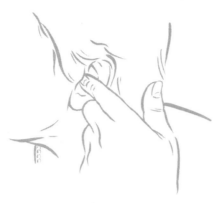

6   Stretch the ear forward to stimulate the back of the ear.

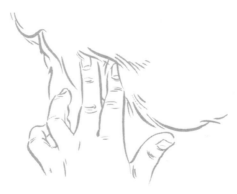

DIY FOOT MASSAGE TO IMPROVE CIRCULATION

Reflexology is an ancient Chinese massage technique based on the principle that nerve centres in the feet are directly connected to other parts of the body. Massaging these nerve centres – known as reflexes – can pinpoint problems in various organs. Working on these tender spots, with tiny movements, stimulates the nerves that connect to the problem organs.

This massage gives very strong control of inner harmony and improves your circulation, which encourages all your systems to work more effectively. When we are getting older and during menopause, we can have problems with the lymph system. Chemicals in the body slow down, thickening the lymph and creating stagnation within the tissue, which leads to slow degeneration within the body. This massage, which should take around five minutes on each foot, will boost circulation, improve digestion and encourage the elimination of water retention and abdominal bloating, while raising energy levels and enhancing sexual vitality. It also has a balancing effect on hormonal activity, and is useful for treating PMT if you are still menstruating. Direct stimulation of the feet will also help to relieve aches, pains and swelling in the legs, ankles, heels and feet.

Begin on the weakest foot, the one that feels more tender to the touch and remember that a foot massage should not stop at the feet; always extend the work up the ankle.

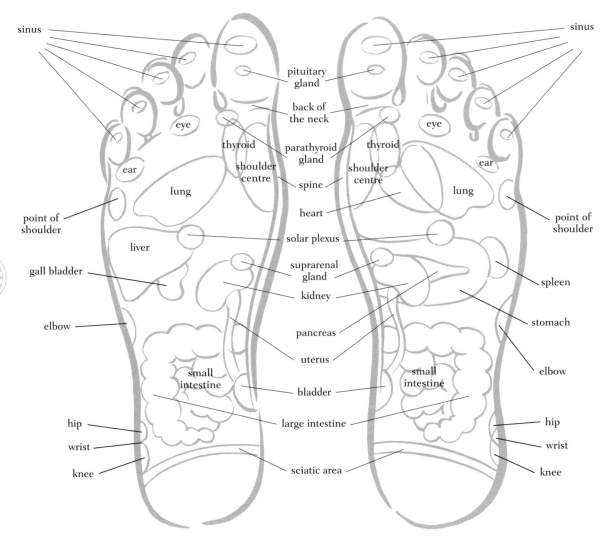

the reflexology zones

sinus

sinus

pituitary
gland

back of
the neck

eye

parathyroid
gland

thyroid

thyroid

eye

shoulder
centre

shoulder
centre

ear

spine

ear

lung

heart

lung

point of
shoulder

point of
shoulder

liver

solar plexus

suprarenal
gland

gall bladder

spleen

kidney

elbow

stomach

pancreas

elbow

uterus

small
intestine

small
intestine

bladder

hip

large intestine

hip

wrist

wrist

knee

sciatic area

knee

1 Press on these three points and move your fingers upwards, maintaining a deep pressure to encourage improved circulation.

2 The area surrounding the inner ankle bone is very important. Make deep finger ball pressure to stimulate the spleen and kidney meridians, which are very important points in Chinese medicine. Applying acupressure here leads to detoxification, helps to remove waste products, gives good hormonal balance, and allows the tissues to work better. Working on the inside of the ankle can also ease dryness of the vagina and help decrease high blood pressure.

3   If the inside of the leg is too sensitive, keep working, but decrease the pressure as you move your fingers up the leg to a point four finger widths above the tip of the ankle bone. Be careful to avoid bruising yourself. Even working gently on the thinner skin on this very powerful acupoint is beneficial, as it is the meeting point of the spleen, liver and kidney meridians. It tones and strengthens the gynaecological organs and helps to keep them in position.

4   The base of the fleshy part of the underside of your foot is a good acupressure pump and is found in the depression just below the ball of the foot. Pressing deeply for up to a minute, and letting go several times helps to invigorate the circulation, promotes vitality, helps to balance blood pressure, and is a good treatment for older people as it increases blood flow to all areas.

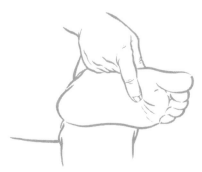

5   This is splint 6, in Chinese medicine it is recognized as the strongest
    point for controlling the hormones. To find it, mark out your four fingers
    from the ankle bone as a guide. Press your thumb into the point using
    deep pressure before letting go. Repeat this several times. Working on
    the outside of the ankle can also benefit the ovaries.

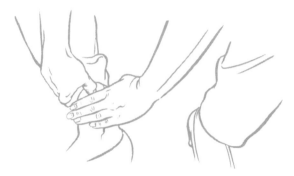

6   The area surrounding the bone is very important, and can help to reduce
    high blood pressure. Use concentrated deep finger ball pressure.

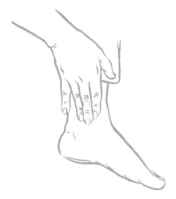

7   These points are very important for blood pressure. Press with quite a
     deep pressure, and then drag your fingers away to give a boost to your
     circulation. Working on the front of the foot also improves liver function
     and boosts the immune system. Pull your fingers firmly along the top of
     the foot to intercept the nerve junction. Repeat this process to relieve the
     effects of stress and toxins in the body, and regulate blood pressure.

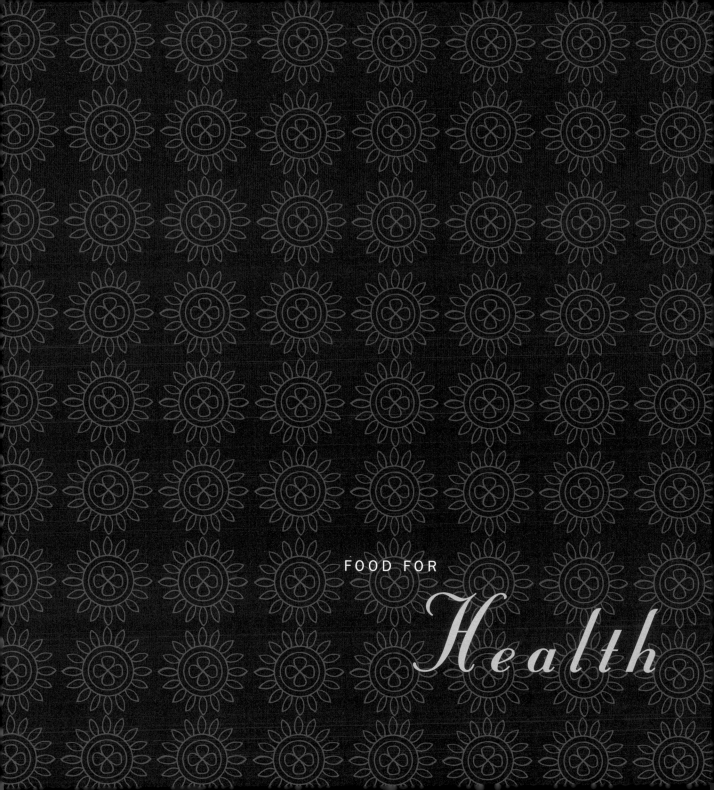

FOOD FOR

Health

If you want a healthy body, you must

Eat to Enjoy ... Eat to Stay Young!

The food you choose becomes you. There is no source of building materials for skin, bones, nerves and other body tissues other than the food you place in your mouth. If you want a healthy body, eat a healthy diet.

In this section I want to explain what I mean by a healthy diet, and show you how you can prepare dishes that take very little time in the kitchen, and are full of flavour. Our modern lives keep us busy, and we all need a diet that is practical, delicious and beautiful to smell and taste. As with all my work, I turn to my Indian upbringing for inspiration, and base these suggestions on foods enjoyed in that country. Many of the recipes in this section were created for western tastes, but they all have oriental origins. They are light, and not overly spicy.

Also, they are based on foods packed with slow-release energy from complex carbohydrates. As the body digests lentils, beans and other pulses, a steady flow of energy enters the bloodstream. This will keep you

Did you know...

Sesame seeds are a rich source of calcium.

first have a healthy and balanced diet

going for a long time, unlike the quick-energy lift you get after eating sweets and drinks filled with carbohydrate in the form of purified sugar.

Eastern foods are far higher than their western counterparts in nutrients that help our bodies fight disease and slow down degenerative changes. The mixtures of fresh fruits, vegetables, grains and pulses (legumes) supply all the vital minerals we need and, with the exception of vitamin B12, all our vitamins. As the bacteria in our gut is a natural source of B12, the fact that Indian food helps maintain a healthy digestive system protects that nutrient as well.

We often overlook the amazing quality of nutrition in simple foods like peas, nuts and rice. All the grains, nuts and pulses (legumes) are life-bearing foods. That is, they all contain the embryo of a new plant and all the nutrients needed to make that tiny new plant grow. For that reason, they are an excellent source of minerals, vitamins, proteins and essential unsaturated fats for our bodies as well.

I am a vegetarian, and I know that the food I eat never leaves me without adequate protein. As for energy, the same grains and pulses (legumes) and root vegetables that I eat for protein contain enough slow-release energy to keep me going all day. My recipes are all low in fat. None includes red meat, because that is one of the primary sources of saturated fat in food. If you eat red meat, I suggest you use it in small amounts, enjoying the flavour but keeping the fat to a minimum.

As we age, our bodies need gentle care. That goes for what we put inside as well as how we take care of what is outside. I do not recommend curries that are too hot. I think we tend to overdo things. In this chapter I give you thirty recipes; almost all contain chilli – even some of the fruit recipes are given zing with this nutrient-packed spice. However, I use just a little bit. You can increase the amount if you like, but never do anything to excess.

Each cell in our bodies needs to be fe

I also think there is too much stress on citrus fruit in our diet. Mangoes, melons, papayas, apricots and all the easy-to-eat fruits we have in the markets today are easy on your stomach and, I believe, better for you. Many people think they need to eat citrus fruit because it is the best source of vitamin C; this is not true. The simple pepper has many more times the amount of vitamin C (weight for weight) than the flesh from an orange.

Medical research has told us by experimentation what we cooks have known for centuries: there are some foods that have very strong healing powers. In the margins throughout the book you will find pieces of information about various ingredients used in Indian cooking and what they can do for your body. But there are three major new ideas about substances in food that so important I want to highlight them here. These ideas are summed up in the words: *antioxidants*, *phytochemicals*, and *micronutrients*. They sound technical, but they are not. Look at it this way.

The body consists of billions of cells, each of which is independently carrying out a number of internal chemical processes at the same time. It is rather like each cell is a tiny chemical factory. If these factories have all the raw materials they need for every part of every process, things run smoothly. If every cell can send off to other cells all of the goods it has 'manufactured' – energy, hormones and enzymes – then everything runs smoothly. If every cell can get rid of all the waste accumulated during its work, then things run smoothly. When things run smoothly, the body is healthy.

However, nothing runs smoothly all the time. If we are missing key minerals and vitamins in our diet, needed to keep the chemical processes in our cells active and in balance, things will go astray. Classed together, vitamins and minerals are called *micronutrients*, and we now know that the western diet may not provide all we need. Specifically, many of us are

Did you know...

Microwave cooking destroys less vitamin C than conventional stove-top methods.

S
i
m
p
l
y

(149)

R
a
d
i
a
n
t

with the raw materials to do its job

not getting enough selenium, zinc, vitamin C, vitamin E and essential fatty acids, plus other vitamins and minerals. As a result, we slowly develop symptoms that tell us the chemical systems in our cells are not functioning properly. Poor immunity, wrinkled and dry skin, aching joints – even cancer and heart disease have been traced by medical science back to a lack of adequate amounts of key nutrients in the foods we eat. When you enjoy food based on the traditional Indian diet, your body is receiving a rich supply of vitamins and minerals.

Let us return to the chemical processes in cells and talk about antioxidants. Let us say that there is suddenly a bombardment of the cell from outside. Something abnormal enters the cells and disrupts their normal processes. That is what happens when large numbers of highly active molecules called 'free radicals' enter the cells. Let me say that not all free radicals are bad; many normal biological processes cannot work without them, but in excess, they can, over time, actually be fatal. Again, medical research suggests that these substances, in excess, can disrupt the normal working of the body and initiate conditions leading to heart disease and cancer. Excess free radicals are created by environmental pollution, smoking, stress, radiation, even some of the medication we take; the list goes on and on. What can we do about it?

The answer is – eat lots of foods rich in natural antioxidants, which are vitamins C and E, and beta-carotene, a substance the body uses to manufacture vitamin A. The thing to remember is that beta-carotene is actually a better antioxidant than vitamin A. Carotenes are part of the colour system in plants, so fill your plate with fruits and vegetables rich in colour: yellow, red, orange and green. Mangoes, peppers, apricots, cabbage and broccoli. One more thing, these antioxidants need certain minerals to work, so make certain you include nuts in your diet, especially brazil nuts,

Beans, rice, pulses contain powerful

as they contain selenium, an important part of the natural antioxidant system your body uses to mop up and destroy damaging free radicals.

For a last time, go back to the idea of billions of cells carrying out thousands of chemical processes so we can think about phytochemicals. Sometimes stocks of manufactured goods build up – oestrogen molecules, for example. Or sometimes, the machinery wears down a bit and needs a boost. We now know that there are other substances in plants, together called phytochemicals, which are not part of any specific function mapped into the normal working of human cells. However, these substances correct the machinery, balance the machinery, tie up and get rid of excess chemicals that could cause damage. Aspirin is a phytochemical, and just think how important that is when we feel unwell. Soya beans, rice, pulses (legumes) and all the members of the Brassica family of plants contain powerful substances that help kill off dangerous cells, and stimulate processes in the body that may be slowing due to age. Phytochemicals are nothing new, of course, they are getting mentioned in the press now because scientists have better equipment to identify and measure them. These substances have been helping people stay healthy since we began eating soya beans and tofu, and making steaming bowls of rice and dal for our families, and mixing cabbage and onions and garlic into the meat and vegetable dishes we enjoy together at the evening meal.

In other words, the good basic ingredients in Indian food are excellent sources of all the nutrients we need to stay healthy and young in body and spirit.

Did you know...

Tofu, apricots and prunes are good sources of calcium. Enjoy these in your diet for strong bones and healthy muscles.

substances that kill dangerous cells

Chillies: A New World fruit, not known in Asia before the seventeenth century.

Fresh Coriander (Cilantro) The most widely used fresh herb in the world. A native of the Middle East, it is said to reduce stomach upset. To keep the herb fresh for a number of days, buy with roots, if possible. Pour a little water in a plastic bag suspended in a glass or cup; place the coriander (cilantro) in the bag, roots down, and store at the bottom of the refrigerator.

Ginger: You cannot cook Asian food without ginger. Excellent with fish or red meat, and works in harmony with garlic. Ginger is not a root, but a rhizome, or underground stem able to sprout buds. Added to food, or eaten alone, it aids digestion and is effective against many forms of motion sickness and nausea. Place fresh ginger in damp sand to encourage the growth of buds; these are far more tender than the main root, and can be chopped fine before adding to food. Peel before using.

Garlic: Originally a native of Central Asia, garlic is a staple ingredient in most East Asian cooking. Respected for its curative properties, garlic is said to boost the immune system, lower cholesterol levels, and provide powerful natural antioxidants to help fight damaging free radicals.

Tamarind: Excellent in curries and pickles, the seed pods of the tamarind tree add a sour, prune-like flavour to food. Do not let that description turn you away from this delicious food: combined with other ingredients, it adds a unique and excellent flavour. Tamarind is rich in vitamins and said to be a tonic for the kidneys and liver.

Sweet Potato: A food from the New World, these sweet-tasting root vegetables probably arrived in Asia before Columbus discovered America, during the westward travels of pre-Inca natives from Peru.

Sweet potatoes spoil faster than most other root crops, and should eaten within a fortnight of purchase.

Mung Beans (Moong Beans): A native of India, this is the second most commonly used bean in Asia, after the soya bean. Several colours of bean exist, but the black mung bean (*urd dal*) is the most highly prized in India. With the husks removed, beans are sold whole or split, like peas.

Soya Beans (soy beans): The most commonly used bean in Asia, soya provides good quality protein and a host of nutrient compounds. Recent medical research suggests the oestrogen-like substances in this food reduce the unpleasant side effects of menopause, and may help protect against breast cancer.

Coconut Milk: Used widely in stews, soups, drinks and sweets throughout southern Asia, coconut milk is an important source of food energy. Often mistaken for the fluid inside coconuts, the milk is actually made by grating, soaking and squeezing the flesh of the coconut. The fat comes to the top of the milk, and can be skimmed to make a vegetable 'cream'. Canned coconut milk is a handy ingredient to keep on hand.

Apricots: A rich source of beta-carotene, folic acid and iron. Enjoy when they are brightly coloured. Sulphur is added to some dried fruit to preserve its natural colour, and this can be washed off by rinsing several times in warm water (superfood).

Avocado Pears: Rich in potassium and the vital antioxidant triad: vitamins A, C and E, which block damage by harmful free-radicals. They also contain easily digested monounsaturated fats, like those found in olive oil. The pulp of the avocado is thought to contain antifungal and antibacterial compounds, and substances that stimulate collagen development in skin, thus increasing its smoothness and elasticity (superfood).

Did you know...

Your body manufactures vitamin A from beta-carotene, which is found in carrots, red and orange peppers, apricots, green leafy vegetables and all other green, red and yellow fruits and vegetables.

Simply

153

Radiant

Crucifers: Scientific evidence shows that green plants of the *Crucifer* family, especially the sub-group known as the *Brassicas*, contain powerful anti-cancer substances. Including more of these foods in our diet may be one of the best means of preventing cancer, so make sure you enjoy at least one portion of the following each day: broccoli, cauliflower, cabbage, kale, Brussels sprouts, turnips, mustard greens and kohlrabi. Broccoli is also a good source of iron.

Cabbage: A rich source of iron, cabbage is thought to help prevent certain cancers.

Dates: An excellent source of fruit sugars, dates are an ideal addition to packed lunches. They are a good source of minerals needed for good health, and aid the digestive system by acting as a mild laxative.

Garlic: Garlic is a healing food known to contain natural antifungal, antibacterial and antiviral compounds. Research suggests that garlic helps reduce blood cholesterol levels, lower blood pressure and prevent abnormal blood clots. It also contains a substance that aids the uptake of oxygen by cells of the body.

Lentils: These members of the pulse (legume) family contain good quantities of B-complex vitamins, iron and protein. To enhance the absorption of iron from lentils, be sure to include a food rich in vitamin C – such as peppers – at the same meal. Lentils are high in 'purines', and should be avoided by people with gout.

Melons: These fruits gently stimulate the kidneys, and aid in a cleansing diet.

Milk and Dairy Products: These are good sources of protein, calcium and B-complex vitamins. However, dairy foods, especially from cows, are not easy for everyone to digest. Especially in Asia and parts of the southern hemisphere, many people lack the digestive enzymes needed to break down milk prior to absorption from the gut, and find digestive

Did you know...

Milk and other dairy products fortified with vitamins are good value, as they contain the vitamin D needed to absorb the calcium present.

problems disappear when this food is eliminated from their diet. If you find your digestion improves after eliminating cows' milk products from your diet, but would like to enjoy some form of cheese or milk drink, try products made from ewes' milk and goats' milk.

A QUICK GUIDE TO AGE-DEFYING NUTRIENTS

All essential nutrients help keep you youthful and healthy. However, the following substances are especially useful to the mature body.

WHAT THEY ARE	WHAT THEY DO	WHERE TO FIND THEM
Micronutrients		
Calcium	Muscle activity, normal blood clotting, strong teeth and bones.	Dairy products, soya beans, lentils, sesame seeds, green leafy vegetables and tinned sardines.
Iron	Keeps up energy levels. Helps blood to carry oxygen to cells.	Wholegrains, apricots, figs, meat (liver), canned sardines, green leafy vegetables.
Beta-carotene	Powerful antioxidant that neutalizes damaging free radicals. Protects against certain forms of cancer. Protects the skin against early deterioration. Helps to protect the heart and prevent certain forms of age-related blindness.	Yellow and orange fruits and vegetables. Green leafy vegetables.

WHAT THEY ARE	WHAT THEY DO	WHERE TO FIND THEM
Vitamin E	Powerful antioxidant. Helps prevent free radical damage to the skin and other tissues. Protects against heart disease.	Nuts, seeds, vegetable oils, avocado.
Vitamin C	Needed to form collagen, the substance that gives skin elasticity and a youthful appearance. Works with vitamin A to deactivate damaging free radicals. Strengthens teeth and gums. Gum disease is the most common reason for the loss of teeth in people over 35. Boosts the immune system. Helps control the nervous system. Aids the absorption of iron from vegetable sources.	Blackcurrants, strawberries, peppers, potatoes, citrus fruit, cabbage.
Selenium	Helps prevent heart disease and cancer. Works with vitamins C and A to protect against the harmful activity of free radicals.	Brazil nuts, wholegrain cereals, lentils, dairy foods, red meat.
Zinc	Helps fight infection by	Nuts, red meat, shellfish,

WHAT THEY ARE	WHAT THEY DO	WHERE TO FIND THEM
	boosting the immune system. Needed for enzyme activity in the body.	sea vegetables.
B-complex vitamins	Necessary for a healthy nervous system; help fight signs of emotional stress and fatigue. Some vitamins in this group aid the production of red blood cells and help release energy from food.	Nuts, pulses (legumes), wholegrain cereals, soya beans, lean red meat, fortified cereals.
Folate (a member of the B-complex group with special significance)	Needed for normal cell development. Prevents spina-bifida. Required for protein formation by the body. Recent research shows it also helps to prevent heart disease.	Apricots, broccoli, Brussels sprouts, yams, cereals, nuts, wheatgerm, asparagus, avocado.
Essential Fatty Acids (overleaf)	**Vital building blocks in every body cell. Important part of many chemical systems in the body. Help regulate hormones.**	

WHAT THEY ARE	WHAT THEY DO	WHERE TO FIND THEM
Omega 6: linoleic acid	Omega 6: linoleic acid A precursor of gama-linolenic acid, or GLA, used by many women to help control the unpleasant symptoms of menstruation and menopause. Also strengthens nails and hair, and protects skin collagen from breakdown by free radicals.	Seed oils, seeds, linseed, nuts.
Omega 3: linolenic acid	Helps maintain normal blood fat levels and therefore protects the heart and vascular system. Helps control joint inflammation. Usually associated with fish oil, but also found in plants, including algae.	Walnuts, linseed, oily fish, algae products.

Other Nutrients

Fibre (soluble)	Helps control blood fat levels, protecting the heart and vascular system.	Oats, wholegrain foods, fruits, vegetables.
Fibre (insoluble)	Stimulates healthy activity of the gut, and prevents constipation.	Bran, pulses (legumes), seeds, grains, vegetables consisting of stems (such as celery).

WHAT THEY ARE	WHAT THEY DO	WHERE TO FIND THEM
Anti-cancer compounds	Medical research has identified certain plants rich in natural plant compounds (phytochemicals, or associate nutrients) that fight cancer. Some of these compounds prevent cancer cells from dividing and spreading. Others stop cancer-causing compounds from entering delicate cells. Identifying these compounds may be the biggest breakthrough we have in the fight against this major killer disease.	By enjoying at least one of the following foods every day, you can give your body a substantial boost against future disease. Remember: they do not all contain the same cancer-fighting compounds, so combine them in salads, soups and stews: soya beans and products, cabbage, broccoli, Brussels sprouts, kohlrabi, tomato purée (paste), tomato sauce and other foods containing cooked tomatoes. The red pigments in tomatoes are powerful antioxidants, thought to fight both cancer and heart disease. Tomatoes must be cooked before this substance is activated, so choosing concentrated tomato products gives you the best quantities of these valuable compounds called lycopenes.
Plant oestrogens (phytoestrogens)		Soya beans and soya products, yams.

BHARTI'S EATING PLAN

This is how I eat, and I recommend it to you. You will see that it is designed for a busy person, who eats at her desk most days. You will also see that it includes a semi-detox, or cleaning diet on one day, and some days when I chose a few foods just because I enjoy them. You cannot be strict with yourself all the time: sometimes you should allow yourself a treat. The basic plan is:

Semi-detox menu (Monday)
Transition menu (Tuesday)
Normal diet (Wednesday, Thursday, Friday)
Weekend menu (Saturday and Sunday)

MONDAY

This is a purification diet, containing no wheat. After the weekend, we want foods that are light.

Breakfast: I start my day with a cup of tea made in the Indian way; sweet with sugar and milk, and flavoured with spices (*see recipe on page* 179). I enjoy this Indian tea with a cereal made of rice and chickpea flour.

Mid-morning: About 10am I eat a piece of fruit. This can be fresh or dried, as long as it is easy to eat. Apples are my favourites, but I make sure to eat yellow and orange varieties as well. Mangoes are always a delicacy. Fruit gives you an energy boost and will carry you through the rest of the morning by keeping the body working slowly and constantly.

Lunch: This must be a practical meal. A sandwich made with rye bread, or other bread – but no wheat. On Monday, the filling can be made of cottage cheese or tofu.

Main meal: This always includes a rice-based dish, served with a vegetable dish and lentils. With this we drink lassi, a dilute yogurt drink that aids digestion. The meal is concluded with more fresh fruit.

TUESDAY

We begin to return to a standard diet, but slowly.

Breakfast: Today, I enjoy wheat toast with Indian tea. I enjoy two or three slices of either white or brown. I like white bread. This diet contains plenty of roughage, so brown bread is not strictly necessary. I also enjoy a little butter on my bread. The portion I use is small, but I will not substitute anything else for it. It is one of my small pleasures. To eat well, you do not have to give up all the things you like.

Mid-morning: Fresh fruit.

Lunch: Sandwich. Vegetable and Cheese Sandwich (*see page 187*).

Main meal: This is a full meal, with lentils, rice, chapattis and dal. Enjoy lassi, but drink water too. Not enough is said about the importance of pure water in the diet. We are very much a water drinking family, and always have a brass jug of water on our table. To finish the meal, enjoy fruit, or an Indian sweet, perhaps one made of dried fruit and nuts. Again, enjoy a small piece. These meals are quite filling, and you should eat only as long as your body feels comfortable.

WEDNESDAY

Breakfast, the mid-morning snack, and lunch are the same as Tuesday. But, for lunch, along with your sandwich, make sure you enjoy some dried fruit. Dried mango slices are delicious, and a good source of beta-carotene. Dried apricots contain beta-carotene and are a rich source of potassium and folate. If you are planning a pregnancy, make sure you eat foods rich in folate.

Main meal: the same as before. We usually have a chickpea or moong dal. We use different pulses because they contain different combinations of amino acids, for making proteins in the body. Also, because different pulses have different textures, they add variety to food. Moong beans are very light on the stomach. Even people who are ill can enjoy and digest moong beans. High in protein and carbohydrates, they are a healing food. Again, the evening meal is finished with refreshing fruit, which should be eaten slowly and enjoyed with the family as they discuss their day.

THURSDAY

Breakfast: Tea and toast, as before.

Midday: A piece of fruit.

Lunch: For a change, enjoy a bean pâté (hummus would do) with rice cakes or bread.

Main meal: This meal includes a soup. Soups can be very filling, but easy to make. The vegetables will be different at this meal. We eat a lot of green vegetables. We eat two types of green vegetables: those with, and those without, seeds. Sometimes we use young beans, which have not yet formed seeds, and other times we use the older beans with seeds in the pods. These have differing nutrient contents, and a combination of the two gives you a full meal.

FRIDAY

Breakfast: Same as before.

Lunch: As before, sandwich or salad.

Main meal: On this day, we use heavier pulses. Black beans, for example. The main dishes are followed by fruit desserts.

SATURDAY AND SUNDAY

We spoil ourselves at the weekend. I must work during the day, but in the evening, and on Sunday, I like to cook for the family. My husband will always have meat, but I prepare dishes where I can enjoy a healthy diet and not eat exactly the same food he does. This is similar to the British tradition of enjoying a Sunday roast.

Fried foods include pori and chapattis. On Saturday evening, it is quite usual for me to make parantha with potatoes, or peas and potatoes. If we are going out, I don't mind eating anything, because it is Saturday.

Sunday morning, we may have our usual food, or a dish made with chick-peas. This is often enjoyed with cabbage.

Sunday lunch: I cook little things all day long; these are very different from what I cook during the week. I fix cassava: boil it, then sprinkle it with a little olive oil, and serve it with chopped green chillies. It is excellent. Or I fry the cassava and serve it with tamarind chutney. Sunday is a family day, so I keep different things coming from the kitchen all the time. I make sure I cook something with my grandchildren. That way, I can show them how to enjoy the foods that will keep them active and feeling good.

So you see, a good healthy diet is easy and varied. Enjoy.

Did you know...

Cabbage is an excellent

source of vitamin C.

Nuts, dried fruit and special flours are

The Recipes

We now come to a section full of delicious recipes for you to cook yourself. They are all based on foods that I cook at home, and my heartfelt thanks go to Jeannette Ewin, who has patiently worked to turn my haphazard handfuls and pinches into accurate recipes, so you can replicate these wonderful, health-giving and sustaining foods at home.

If you have not cooked Indian food before, please begin by visiting an Asian market. You will find it is a treasure trove of vegetables and fruits not available in the regular supermarkets. Bags of nuts, dried fruit, special flours, spices and herbs used in Asian cooking are there for you to explore and enjoy. The chilled cabinets are packed with wonderful drinks, yogurt, cheese and prepared foods that will really excite you. And remember, when prepared the way I say, there is very little fat or oil in most things, so you are shopping for a healthy diet.

The following are a few basic recipes. Every Asian cook has her own way of preparing food, but these ideas will get you started, and then you can try things for yourself. Some of these recipes are not traditional Asian ones, but are excellent ways to follow my diet suggestions anyway.

all types of Asian food to be enjoyed

Basic Recipes

CURRY POWDER
(THE ESSENTIAL BLEND OF HEALING SPICES)

You can buy curry powder, but if you make your own you will soon find it gives your food something special. It is worth the effort. The flavours are fresh, and the ingredients have lost none of their precious essential oils, which carry the unique flavour and aroma of each. You will enjoy the simple pleasure of watching the colour and smell of the curry develop as you work. You should buy a special spice grinder for this, as using a mortar and pestle takes too long.

The ingredients in a very basic curry powder are two parts coriander to one part turmeric. Other ingredients vary by custom, region, and caste in India. In addition to turmeric and coriander, the most common ingredients are: chilli, cumin, cardamom, cloves, nutmeg, black mustard seed, cinnamon, salt and black pepper. The choice of spices is influenced also by the main ingredient: fish, meat, vegetarian dishes, and so on, each require a slightly different blend of spices. Additions to the basic blend may include garlic, onions, ginger, cloves, nutmeg, mace, cardamom (green and black, which looks like dried beetles), cinnamon, tamarind, fennel, fenugreek, caraway, asafoetida and even ginseng! Asafoetida (heeng) is a foul-smelling resin that you should buy already ground, as it is very hard. Do not let the smell put you off: heeng is excellent for the digestion, and is one source of the authentic flavour we enjoy in Indian food. Spices, both whole and ground, are stored in fragrant boxes, and the contents are often shared among members of a family, or friends.

The essential herb in Indian cooking is fresh coriander (cilantro). Be extravagant with it: it is so good for you.

Nutmeg and mace are spices from the same plant. Although nutmeg is thought to reduce discomfort from gastric problems, including vomiting and diarrhoea, it should be used in moderation. Large amounts can cause drowsiness and hallucinations.

DAL

Dried peas, beans and various forms of lentils are collectively referred to as 'dals'. For most Indians, dishes based on these foods, when served with rice, supply the majority of the protein in their diet, so dal is included in most meals. Again, recipes are countless, with every cook seeming to bring her own unique character to each dish. Dal is an excellent dish for slow-release energy – the best kind for your body.

For a basic dal, soak the beans or lentils for two to six hours in water. The length of time depends on the dal. Most should be soaked for one or two hours, but soya and red kidney beans should be soaked overnight. Drain. Add fresh water to the pot, and cook slowly until it is no longer possible to detect individual pieces of food. Do not allow the food to burn, but cook until it is close to dry. Then add ground turmeric, ground coriander and salt. After that, you will soon be creating your own dishes. Dals can be eaten as soups or pâtés, or even used to fill Indian breads. They can be served alone, or with various vegetables added: onions and garlic, for example. Yogurt and vegetable dishes, called raitas, and chutneys go well with these versatile and highly nutritious foods.

(Remember: if you plan to use red kidney beans, called rajma dal in India, they require more care than other beans because they contain a potentially toxic substance. Soak them overnight, change the water, then boil them for an hour. Change the water again and boil until they are soft. Or, if you prefer to do it the convenient way, use canned kidney beans.)

A pressure cooker makes quick work of a dal: just follow the instructions provided with your pan for cooking dried beans and lentils. Do not add seasoning while the dal is in the pressure cooker. Once it is cooked, transfer it to a regular pan, and then add the spices and vegetables. Add a little liquid, if needed, and cook over a low heat for another 10 minutes to allow the flavours to blend.

BASIC DAL WITH A SPICY TARKA

Serves 4

Ingredients

1 litre/35fl oz/4^1/$_2$ cups cold water

255g/9oz/1 cup any dal, washed, soaked and drained

1 tsp ground turmeric

2 tsp ground coriander

1 tsp salt

For the Tarka:

1 tsp cumin seeds

1 garlic clove, minced

1 dried red chilli, crushed

1 tbsp tomato purée (paste)

1 tbsp ghee, or corn oil

1   Bring the water to a boil in a large, heavy pan, and add the dal, turmeric and coriander. Cook, covered, over medium heat, until the dal is tender and can be mashed easily with the back of a spoon. Add the salt. Salt can make the skin on some types of dal tough, so add after they are cooked and soft. Remove the pan from the heat, and allow to stand for at least 15 minutes. This is important, as the dal reabsorbs any excess moisture.

2   While the dal cools, combine the ingredients for the Tarka in a small pan and cook over low heat until fragrant. Do not allow the garlic to brown, as it will become bitter.

3   Stir the Tarka into the dal and serve at once.

4   Dals can be served with a little lemon or ginger pickle to aid digestion.

Turmeric has been used for centuries as a liver tonic and to relieve digestive problems. Like many other spices used in Indian cooking, turmeric contains natural antibacterial compounds that help the body fight infection.

Cardamom sweetens the breath when chewed, stimulates digestion, relieves the symptoms of indigestion and can help calm vomiting.

I suggest removing all seeds from chillies because I think they are hard to digest, and contain most of the heat of the pepper. The fleshy part contains the useful nutrients.

Ginger is a highly therapeutic food. It helps calm the digestion, prevent motion sickness and nausea, and stimulate circulation of the blood.

Sweet peppers are an excellent source of vitamin C, beta-carotene and bioflavonoids.

VARIATIONS:

Moong dal

If you are using moong beans, add cloves and some black cardamom. Moong dal, the tiny green beans most often used to make bean sprouts, is a favourite throughout India. The nutritional value can be enhanced by adding about half a pound of fresh spinach or a cup of thinly sliced Brussels sprouts to a dal made with a cup of split beans. Add the vegetables after the beans are cooked. Cover and allow to cook for another 5 minutes. Adjust the basic Tarka (*see above*) by adding ⅛ tsp black cardamom, a pinch of ground cloves and a pinch of heeng.

MY SPECIAL DAL

This is an easy dish with many health benefits. Canned beans are used to avoid the long soaking and cooking times required by the dried variety.

Serves 4

Ingredients

1 can/425g/14oz cooked chickpeas (garbanzo beans)

1 can/425g/14oz cooked soya beans (soy beans)

squeeze of lemon juice

3 tbsp corn oil or ghee

1 tsp cumin seeds

1 tsp ground coriander

1 large onion, finely chopped

1 large red pepper, seeded and chopped

1 tsp finely chopped fresh root ginger

2 large garlic cloves, minced

1 large green chilli, seeded and finely chopped

black pepper from 6 to 8 turns of a large pepper mill

1 tsp salt

1   Empty both cans of beans into a large sieve and rinse well under cold running water. Tap dry and, with the beans still in the sieve, top with the lemon juice and gently shake to distribute the juice.

2   Place the oil, or ghee, and all the spices in a heavy pan and cook over medium heat until the seeds pop and dance in the pan. Add the onion, pepper, ginger, garlic and chilli, and cook until the onions are translucent. Remove the pan from the heat.

3   In a separate pan, combine the beans with three or four tablespoons of water and bring to the boil. Turn down the heat to a simmer, cover the pan tightly, and cook for another 10 minutes. Drain off the excess moisture and mash the beans well.

4   Add the cooked ingredients to the beans and mash again. Season to taste and serve.

PLAIN AND SIMPLE RICE

I use a standard measuring cup to measure my rice, because it is by far the simplest and quickest way, but if you do not have one, measure out 450ml (15fl oz) of rice in a normal measuring jug.

Serves 6

Ingredients
2 cups long-grain rice (Basmati is best)
1 litre /35fl oz/4^1/$_2$ cups water

1   Wash the rice several times, cover with water and allow to stand for at least 15 minutes.

2   Drain the rice and place in a heavy pan with a tight-fitting lid. Add the water. Place the uncovered pan over high heat and bring to the boil.

3   Turn down the heat to very low. Cover the pan and cook for 25 minutes.

Soya is one of the most powerful foods we can eat to protect our health and slow the advance of signs of age. Substances called isoflavones, which are similar to the body's natural oestrogen, are believed to help maintain smooth skin and strong bones, and prevent certain forms of female cancer. Extensive laboratory research done around the world suggests that genistein, protease inhibitors and phytic acids – all compounds found in soya – stop the formation of cancer in its early stages, or actually kill cancer cells. Including some form of soya in your diet every day is a good way to stay healthy for longer.

Garlic is said to be good for the heart and it helps to control cholesterol levels in the blood.

4   Remove the pan from the heat. Do not remove the lid. Leave to cool for at least 10 minutes.

Carrot and Onion Rice

Ingredients

3 tsp corn oil or ghee

1 tsp cumin seeds

1 tsp coriander seeds

1 tsp caraway seeds

1 small onion, chopped

3 tender, young carrots, grated

1 dried red chilli, crushed

1 garlic clove, minced

2 cups long-grain rice (Basmati is best)

1 litre /35fl oz/4$\frac{1}{2}$ cups water

1   Pour the oil into a heavy pan, large enough to cook the rice. Add the spices and cook over medium heat until the seeds pop.

2   Stir in the vegetables, chilli and garlic and cook for about 10 minutes, stirring from time to time, until the vegetables are tender.

3   Add the rice to the pan. Stir and cook for another 3 to 4 minutes. Add the water, cover tightly, and cook as above.

Certain forms of blindness associated with advancing age are less prevalent in cultures that include orange and yellow fruit and vegetables and green leafy food in their diet.

Coconut and Chilli Rice

Serves 4

Ingredients

2 cups long-grain rice (Basmati is best)

650ml/24fl oz/3 cups water

1 can/425g/14oz coconut milk

1 green chilli, seeded and finely chopped

$^1/_2$ tsp ground cloves

$^1/_2$ tsp ground ginger

1   Place all the ingredients in a large, heavy pan with a lid. Place over medium heat and bring to the boil.

2   Reduce to the lowest possible heat, cover and allow to cook – unopened – for 30 minutes.

3   Remove from heat and allow to stand, unopened, for 10 minutes.

4   Stir and serve with dal and raita.

WALNUT AND GINGER CHUTNEY

Ingredients

55g/2oz/$^2/_3$ cup shelled walnuts

$^1/_2$ small dried chilli, torn into pieces

$^1/_4$ tsp salt

1 piece of preserved ginger in syrup

3 tbsp plain yogurt

1   Place the nuts, chilli and salt in a mortar and pound until smooth.

2   Add the ginger and pound again, leaving identifiable pieces of ginger.

3   Pour the mixture into a small bowl, add the yogurt and stir.

4   Cover and refrigerate before use.

Walnuts are a vital source of fats (omega-3 fatty acids) that help maintain a healthy heart, boost the immune system, and protect joints from certain forms of arthritis.

GARLIC AND CHILLI CHUTNEY

This is a powerful chutney that we keep on hand at home. A tiny amount will add character and depth to any dish you are preparing. Try it in dal or rice dishes, and to add depth to your vegetable dishes. This will keep in a jar with a tight-fitting lid in the refrigerator for about a week.

Ingredients

1 tsp salt

3 large garlic cloves

1 tsp chilli powder

a few drops of oil

1   Place the salt, garlic and chilli powder together in a mortar and pound well.

2   Stir in the oil, and scoop into the jar in which you plan to store the chutney.

VARIATION:

To make a powerful dip for crisp, fresh vegetable pieces, blend 2 tablespoons of tomato purée (paste) and an additional tablespoon of oil in to this chutney. WOW!

TOMATO AND CUCUMBER RAITA

The cooling flavour of yogurt goes well with many foods. Made ahead and chilled, this simple salad is a wonderful accompaniment to peppery curry dishes and dals.

Ingredients

2 ripe, medium tomatoes, skinned and chopped (plum tomatoes are best)

$^1/_2$ large cucumber, peeled and shredded

1 cup yogurt (Greek-style yogurt gives excellent results.)

1 tsp ground cumin

pinch of asafoetida (optional)

salt and black pepper

fresh mint, chopped, to garnish

1   Prepare the tomatoes and cucumbers and allow them to drain in a sieve to remove excess moisture.

2   In a bowl, combine the yogurt and spices. Stir well.

3   Add the drained vegetables to the mixture, and gently combine by turning over two or three times with a wooden spoon. Season to taste.

4   Refrigerate for at least 2 hours before serving. Garnish with chopped mint.

Asafoetida (heeng) is used in several systems of healing. It subdues wind and nasal mucus, and is said to increase the appetite. It aids gastric processes, strengthens the heart and regulates the menstrual cycle. It is also a tonic for the liver and spleen, and can be used in the treatment of rheumatism, deafness, paralysis and eye disease. In other words, don't let its smell put you off. A tiny amount of heeng in your food each day helps you stay young.

Simply

175

Radiant

TOASTED NUTS

This recipe is simplicity itself.

Ingredients

raw walnuts or pecans

salt

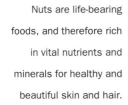
Nuts are life-bearing
foods, and therefore rich
in vital nutrients and
minerals for healthy and
beautiful skin and hair.

1   Spread your raw walnuts or pecans evenly over a large baking sheet.
    Place in a cold oven and set the temperature to 150°C/300°F/Gas 2.

2   After fifteen minutes, stir the nuts and sprinkle liberally with salt. When
    you begin to smell the aroma of the nuts, check their colour. Continue to
    toast only until they have reached a golden colour.

3   Remove from the oven and allow to cool. Pour the toasted nuts into a bowl
    or air-tight container for storage, shaking off any excess salt as you do.

Drinks Recipes

LASSI

Water, beer and wine are not the best drinks to enjoy with spicy Indian food. Yogurt drinks are always best, because they balance the heat in the food and aid digestion. Lassi is made of diluted yogurt and is one of the most popular foods in India. It is easy to digest, and so is excellent for small children and anyone who is pregnant or recovering from an illness. Some people believe no meal is complete until it is finished with a glass of this delicious drink. Lassi can be enjoyed either as a savoury or a sweet drink.

Yogurt is usually made by incubating pasteurized milk with special bacteria. These organisms make the milk easier to digest by partially breaking down the protein. Yogurt is a good source of calcium and phosphorus, and contains useful amounts of Vitamins B2 and B12. It helps boost the immune system, replace bacteria (flora) in the gut killed by antibiotics, and may aid both constipation and diarrhoea. Maintaining normal, healthy flora in the gut may be an important factor in preventing cancer of the colon.

SAVOURY LASSI

Serves 2

Ingredients

125ml/4fl oz/$^1/_2$ cup plain yogurt made with whole milk
285ml/10fl oz/1$^1/_3$ cup cold water (still mineral water is best)
$^1/_4$ tsp salt
$^1/_4$ tsp ground cumin
small pinch of ground coriander

1   Place all the ingredients in a blender and whiz for 2 or 3 seconds.

SWEET LASSI

Mango juice is delicious in this drink, as is apple juice and pear nectar. In my opinion, orange juice is too acidic.

Serves 2

Ingredients

125ml/4fl oz/$^1/_2$ cup plain yogurt made with whole milk
285ml/10fl oz/1$^1/_3$ cup cold fruit juice
a tiny, tiny pinch of salt.

1   Place in a blender and blend, as above.

Simply

Radiant

Use only pure fruit juice or nectar, because they contain the highest quantity of healing nutrients. Avoid drinks made with artificial sweeteners, flavourings and preservatives.

SOYA LASSI

This is not a true lassi, but it provides extra plant oestrogen.

Serves 2

Ingredients

125ml/4fl oz/$^1/_2$ cup unsweetened soya milk

285ml/10fl oz/$1^1/_3$ cups fruit juice (apple and mango are excellent)

1   Pour into a jug and mix.

CHAI

Tea, usually made in a samovar, is part of the way most Indians start their day. We like our tea sweetened with a little sugar, and pungent with spices, especially cinnamon and nutmeg. Busy people rarely have time for the luxury of a samovar, but you can buy some excellent blends of Indian spiced tea in the market, or make it at home.

When I am in a hurry, I rinse out a tea pot with boiling water to warm it, and add enough black tea to make two or three cups. Add a small piece of cinnamon (about an inch), a few cardamom pods, several whole cloves, about ¼ teaspoon of freshly ground nutmeg and 2 teaspoons of sugar. Pour in boiling water, replace the lid on the pot at once, and allow the mixture to brew for about five minutes. At this point, add two or three tablespoons of milk. Stir. The milk helps bind the tannin from the tea, making it more digestible than tea with lemon. Strain the tea into your favourite cups, and enjoy both the aroma and flavour.

Enjoy a soya drink every day. Soya milk is lactose free, and packed with protein and minerals. Fortified soya milk is available, rich in vitamins B12 and D, and as much calcium as an equal quantity of cows' milk. Soya milk is a good source of isoflavonoids, which help reduce the threat of cancer and ease the symptoms of menopause.

Cinnamon helps decongest the nasal passages, and helps prevent flatulence, diarrhoea and indigestion. It is a good tonic for your system at the start of the day.

PEA AND CORN SOUP

This is a slimming soup, and can be enjoyed hot or cold.

Serves 2

Ingredients

1 tbsp corn oil

1 tsp cumin seeds

1 tsp fenugreek

1 large garlic clove, minced

1 green chilli, seeded and finely chopped

1 can/425g/14oz plum tomatoes

1 cup frozen petit pois

1 cup frozen tender corn

$1/2$ litre stock (bouillon) – vegetarian or chicken

$1/4$ small head cabbage (green or white), finely chopped

salt and black pepper to taste

1   Combine the oil, cumin seeds and fenugreek in a soup pot, and heat until the seeds sizzle. Turn down the heat to low, add the garlic and chilli and cook until the garlic begins to brown.

2   Add the tomatoes, peas, corn and stock (bouillon). Stir. Place the cabbage on top of the combined ingredients, cover the pot, and simmer for 20 minutes.

3   Add salt and black pepper to taste, and serve piping hot with dark bread.

Cumin seeds relieve colic and indigestion.

LENTIL SOUP WITH SUN-DRIED TOMATOES

If you use the kind of sun-dried tomatoes that are preserved in oil, drain them well on paper kitchen towelling before use.

Serves 2

Ingredients

115g/4oz/$^1/_2$ cup split red lentils

About a litre/35fl oz/4$^1/_2$ cups water

4 tbsp virgin olive oil

1 small onion, finely chopped

1 large garlic clove, minced

1 tsp black mustard seed

1 small, dried chilli pepper, crushed

1 bay leaf

$^1/_2$ tsp ground cloves

1 tsp ground cumin

4–5 sun-dried tomatoes, cut into small pieces

1 stock (bouillon) cube (vegetarian or chicken), crumbled

salt and black pepper to taste

1   Place the lentils in a large pot or bowl, add the water and allow to soak for at least 15 minutes.

2   Pour the oil into a heavy soup pot over medium heat. Add the onion, garlic, mustard seed and chilli, and stir. Turn the heat down as low as possible, cover the pan and allow to 'sweat'; after 6 or 7 minutes, check to see that the vegetables are cooking, but not burning. Remove from the heat.

3   Carefully add the lentils and water to the mixture of vegetables and oil. Add the bay leaf, cloves and cumin. Place over medium heat and bring to

Mustard seeds are an ancient remedy for headache and flu. Black mustard is hotter than brown.

the boil. Cook for 5 minutes, turn the heat to low, cover and simmer for 30 minutes, stirring once or twice to stop the lentils from sticking.

4   Add the sun-dried tomato pieces and stock (bouillon) cube. Replace the lid and simmer for another half-hour, stirring occasionally. Add more water if necessary.

5   Remove the bay leaf from the soup. Season to taste. Serve with dark rye bread and a little butter.

QUICK BROCCOLI SOUP

Serves 4

Ingredients
1 medium head of broccoli
1 medium onion, quartered
240ml/8fl oz/1 cup water
1 stock (bouillon) cube (vegetable or chicken), crumbled
225g/8 oz/1 cup Greek-style yogurt
1 tsp ground cumin
salt and ground black pepper to taste
fresh coriander (cilantro), finely chopped

1   Remove the outer leaves from the broccoli, wash and remove most of the stem. Break the remaining head into pieces. Combine the broccoli, onion, water and stock (bouillon) cube in a soup pot. Bring to the boil, cover and cook over medium heat until the broccoli is tender.

2   Carefully remove the vegetables and stock to a blender. Add the yogurt and cumin. Cover and whizz. Adjust the consistency of the soup with a little soya milk if it is too thick for your liking. Adjust the flavour with salt and freshly ground black pepper, if necessary.

3   Return the soup to the pot if you plan to reheat it before serving, or
    simply pour into soup plates and sprinkle with the fresh coriander before
    serving.

Broccoli, like all the Brassica plants (which include cabbage, Brussels sprouts and cauliflower), provides vitamins and minerals, powerful antioxidants and natural compounds shown to help fight cancer.

Mid-day Meals

BHARTI'S 'BREAD'

This, of course, is not a true bread, although its characteristics are similar to those of American 'quick breads'. Again, this is a slimming food full of flavour. Serve hot with Gingered Beans with Tomato (*see page 189*), or enjoy cold with Tomato and Cucumber Raita (*see page 175*). A slice stored in a sandwich container makes a delicious lunch-box meal.

Makes 6 servings (this dish is very filling)

Ingredients

2 tbsp corn oil

1 tbsp black mustard seeds

$1^1/_2$ tsp sea salt

$^1/_2$ tsp freshly ground black pepper

1 small chilli, seeded and chopped

1 large onion, chopped

1 large red pepper, seeded and chopped

140g/5oz/1 cup gram flour

240ml/8fl oz/1 cup soya milk (unsweetened)

3 medium eggs, beaten

225g/8oz/1 cup Quark, or other very low-fat soft cheese

1 tbsp garam masala (or commercial curry powder)

1   Preheat the oven to 175°C/325°F/Gas 3. Butter a 23cm (9 in) square baking pan or lasagne dish.

2   Combine the oil, mustard seeds, salt, black pepper and chilli in a heavy frying pan (skillet) and heat until the seeds 'pop'. Add the onion and red pepper, cover and cook until the vegetables are tender.

3   Meanwhile, combine the gram flour and soya milk in a large mixing bowl. Add the eggs gradually. (Gram flour is surprisingly heavy, so the mixture will be thick.)

4   Add the low-fat cheese and mix well to combine. Stir in the cooked vegetables, spices and oil and the garam masala.

5   Pour the mixture into the prepared dish and bake for 30 minutes, or until the centre of the 'bread' is firm.

SANDWICHES

It is said that the Earl of Sandwich originated this convenience food so he could eat without interrupting his gambling. Today, a well-made sandwich is just the thing to sustain a busy woman throughout the day. You may be lucky, and have a really good sandwich shop near you, but many people find they prefer the ones they make at home. Buy a well-built sandwich box, find some filling recipes you enjoy, and relax as you eat a meal that is delicious and packed with goodness.

Choosing the right bread is important, and I go for texture and content. Enjoy breads made with a mixture of grains: pumpernickel, for example. Or, make your sandwich in a wholemeal pitta bread. Obviously, what you chose for a filling must be full of flavour as well as nutritious. Variations on fillings are endless, but try the three listed here and then create your own variations.

On Mondays, you may want to enjoy rice crackers or rye crispbread as the main carbohydrate part of your meal. If so, spoon the sandwich filling into a small jar with a tight lid, pack a spreader in your sandwich box, and enjoy.

Grains, seeds, beans and peas are all rich sources of B-complex vitamins, needed for a calm and healthy nervous system. These are the anti-stress vitamins.

Adequate levels of folate, a member of the B-complex group, are important during the very early stages of pregnancy to prevent the crippling developmental disease, spina-bifida. Folate has also been demonstrated to have a protective effect on the heart.

If it is socially acceptable, add a few thin slivers of raw onion. It is delicious!

Dairy food, brazil nuts and avocados contain selenium, a mineral needed to help protect the body against free radical destruction and premature signs of age.

Avocados and walnuts contain vitamin E, an essential antioxidant vitamin known to protect against the effects of free radicals.

Walnuts are a rich source of vitamins, minerals and natural antioxidants. The essential fatty acids they contain help maintain a healthy heart and vascular system.

AVOCADO, WALNUT AND SOFT CHEESE SANDWICH FILLING

Try this tucked inside a fresh pitta bread.

Makes 2 or 3 hearty sandwiches

Ingredients

1 medium, ripe avocado

1 small green chilli, seeded and very finely chopped

2 tbsp Quark, or other very low-fat soft cheese

black pepper from a few turns of a pepper mill.

pinch of salt

pinch of sugar

1 tbsp toasted walnuts, finely chopped

2 or 3 pitta breads

a few drops of olive oil.

1 ripe tomato, thinly sliced

cress, to garnish (optional)

1 Scoop the flesh from the avocado and place in a medium-sized mixing bowl. Mash in the chilli, cheese, pepper, salt and sugar. Blend well. Stir in the toasted nuts.

2 Cut a thin strip from the edge of a pitta bread and carefully open the pocket. Brush the inside of the bread with the olive oil.

3 Spread the avocado mixture over the thicker side of the pocket, layer in a few slices of tomato, and gently press the pocket closed. A little cress adds texture and nutrients.

VEGETABLE AND CHEESE SANDWICH FILLING

Prepare the vegetables for this sandwich filling ahead of time. This result is delicious, but the pre-assembly work is a bit tedious. Try doing this while you are cooking the evening meal for your family.

Makes 2 hearty sandwiches

Ingredients

olive oil, for frying and rubbing the bread

1 small onion, sliced

$^1/_4$ tsp ground turmeric

1 small aubergine (eggplant), thinly sliced

1 medium red pepper, seeded and cut into strips

salt and black pepper, to taste

2 wholewheat rolls

4 thin slices cheese (try a cheese with 'punch'; Kefalotiri, or perhaps double Gloucester)

1   Use two heavy pans for this. Pour a little oil into each. Put the onion in one pan, turn the heat on low, cover tightly, and allow to cook until the slices begin to turn brown. Stir in the turmeric and place the mixture in a bowl.

2   Meanwhile, space some of the aubergine (egg plant) and pepper out in the second pan so they do not overlap. Cover and cook over low heat for 5 minutes. Turn the vegetables over, sprinkle lightly with salt and pepper, and cook for another 6 or 7 minutes. Remove to paper towels to drain. Repeat this process until all the vegetables are cooked. Place the drained vegetables on a plate or flat dish.

3   When you are ready to make your sandwich, split the rolls and toast them, then rub a little oil over the inside surfaces of each one. (This helps keep the bread from becoming soggy.)

I make batches of fried onions ahead of time and keep them in a tightly covered bowl in the refrigerator. Then, when I am in a hurry, but want to add the flavour of onion to a dish I am preparing, I simply use the onion that is already on hand.

Dietary studies of older people show that they are prone to be deficient in most B vitamins, beta-carotene, vitamin C, and the minerals magnesium, iron and potassium. This sandwich recipe is packed with these nutrients.

Aubergine contains plant compounds that are thought to prevent cancer and act as powerful antioxidants. The best are the small varieties found in Asian markets.

4   To assemble each sandwich, place three or four pieces of pepper and aubergine on the bottom half of the sandwich, add a few strands of onion, and top with a slice or two of cheese. Press the sandwich together, wrap and place in your sandwich box.

Cheese is a good source of calcium.

This is a good way to enjoy tofu; remember, it is one of the foods that fights signs of age.

TOFU AND CHEESE SPREAD

Serves 4

Ingredients

1 package/300g/10^1/$_2$ oz extra-firm tofu

55g/2oz/^{1}/$_2$ cup mature Cheddar cheese, grated

1 large shallot, chopped

85g/3oz/^{1}/$_2$ cup grated young carrot (washed and peeled, unless organic)

1 tbsp soy mayonnaise

1 tsp mustard seeds, toasted

pinch of chilli powder

small pinch of salt

1   Drain the tofu. Place all the ingredients in a food processor or blender and blend.

2   Use at once to make sandwiches, or as a dip with crudités.

Main Dishes

GINGERED BEANS WITH TOMATO

Serves 4

Ingredients

1 can/425g/14oz chopped plum tomatoes

1 small onion, chopped

130g/4^1/$_2$oz/1^1/$_2$ cup frozen broad (fava) beans (peas or French beans may be substituted)

1 stock (bouillon) cube (vegetable or chicken), crumbled

1 tbsp ground ginger

1 tsp sugar

salt and black pepper, to taste

1 tbsp ghee, or butter

1   Combine tomatoes, onion, beans and stock (bouillon) cube in a heavy pan; cover and cook over low heat until the vegetables are soft. Remove the lid, turn up the heat, and, watching carefully, cook the mixture until most of the liquid has evaporated.

2   Add the ginger, sugar and a few 'turns' of freshly ground black pepper.

3   Stir in the ghee, or butter. Adjust the salt and pepper to taste, and serve with plain rice and dal, or with Bharti's bread, hot from the oven.

POTATO AND BRUSSELS SPROUT CURRY

Serves 4

Ingredients

2 tbsp corn oil

1 tbsp mustard seeds

1 tsp coriander seeds

3 medium potatoes, diced

1 large leek, cleaned and sliced into rounds (or a medium sized onion)

1 large green chilli, seeded and finely chopped

pinch of salt

225g/8oz/2 cups Brussels sprouts, finely chopped

2 firm, ripe tomatoes, skinned and sliced

1 tsp ground cumin

1 tbsp ground turmeric

1 Over high heat, pour the oil into a heavy pan with a tight lid. Add the mustard and coriander seeds and cook until the seeds pop. Turn the heat down to low.

2 Place the potatoes, leek, green chilli and salt in the pan. Cover and cook for 10 minutes. Uncover the pan and stir. Spread the Brussels sprouts over the potato mixture. Next, top with the tomato slices. Cover again, leaving over very low heat.

3 Cook for another 20 minutes, but do not allow to burn. Remove the lid, sprinkle the cumin and turmeric over the vegetables and stir. Turn off the heat and allow to stand for another five minutes. Spoon carefully into a dish and serve.

Brussels sprouts are part of the Brassica family, and rich in natural substances that fight cancer. They are also rich in vitamin C and beta-carotene, and are a good source of folate and fibre. Brussels sprouts can cause wind, but cooking them with Indian spices lets you get the best from them without the unwanted side-effects. The best way to prepare Brussels sprouts is to slice them finely before cooking. An uncut sprout tends to be overcooked on the outside and undercooked on the inside.

CHICKEN AND ONION CURRY

Serves 4

Ingredients

1 tbsp lemon juice

3 tbsp corn oil

1 garlic clove, minced

2 green chillies, seeded and thinly sliced

1 tsp ground cumin

1 tsp ground turmeric

455g/1lb fresh, skinless, boneless chicken breast

2 large, sweet onions, very thinly sliced

pinch of salt

1   In a large bowl, combine the lemon juice, 1 tablespoon of the oil, the garlic, chillies, cumin and turmeric.

2   Cut the chicken, crosswise, into thin slices. Add to the bowl and leave to marinate for at least 1 hour.

3   Pour the remaining oil into a heavy frying pan (skillet) over high heat. When the pan is hot, add the chicken, draining off and reserving as much of the marinade as possible. Seal the chicken by frying over the high heat for 1 or 2 minutes, then reduce the heat. Add the marinade with all its spices. Cook until the chicken is tender.

Lycopene, the pigment in tomatoes, has been shown to act as a powerful natural antioxidant protecting us against heart disease and our partners against both heart disease and prostate cancer. Tomatoes must be cooked before lycopene is released from their cells, so canned tomatoes, fresh cooked tomatoes and tomato purée (paste) should be part of your everyday diet.

Vary this dish by using finely cut cabbage instead.

Compounds in onions are thought to reduce blood cholesterol levels, lower blood pressure and prevent blood clots. There is strong evidence that they also are rich in natural antibiotics.

4   While the pan is still over the heat, tip the pan slightly, so that the oil and juices from the chicken run freely. Pull the chicken towards the top of the pan and add the onion to the exposed juice. Return the pan to its normal position, and cook the onions until they are wilted. Remove from the heat and sprinkle with salt. Serve at once with rice and My Special Dal.

EGG AND TOMATO CURRY

Serves 2

Ingredients

3 tbsp corn oil

1 small onion, chopped

1 large green pepper, seeded and chopped

1 tbsp chopped fresh root ginger

1 tsp tamarind paste

1 can/425g/14 oz plum tomatoes

1 tsp ground cinnamon

1 tsp sugar

pinch of salt

4 medium eggs, hard boiled

1 tsp garam masala

2 tbsp chopped fresh coriander (cilantro)

1   Pour the oil in a pan and gently fry the onion, green pepper, ginger and tamarind paste. Add the canned tomatoes and cook until the mixture has lost most of its moisture.

2   Add the cinnamon, sugar and salt. Stir. Gently lower the eggs into the mixture, spooning the sauce over the eggs. Cover and turn down the heat to the lowest possible level.

3   Leave the covered pan over the low heat for 3 or 4 minutes, then remove from the heat. Uncover, add the garam masala and stir. Cover tightly and leave the pan to stand for another 10 minutes before serving.

4   Arrange the eggs and tomato sauce over a plate of plain rice. Sprinkle with the chopped coriander (cilantro) before serving.

Garam masala is a blend of aromatic spices, usually containing cardamom seeds, cumin seeds, cloves, nutmeg, cinnamon and black pepper. There are thousands of variations. The spices and ground and then stored, and sprinkled on food shortly before serving. For busy people, commercial blends are handy. Buy yours at a good Asian market where you know it is authentic.

Tamarind is the sour rind of a long fruit filled with large, hard seeds. It gives a distinctive sour taste of Indian food that is good with eggs or fish. It has a high vitamin C content, and is a mild laxative. Like many Indian foods, it is good for the digestion.

Something for Afters

SPICY MANGO

Mangoes are rich in beta-carotene, a substance the body makes into vitamin A, which is important for healthy skin and essential for a strong immune system. However, on its own, beta-carotene is a powerful nutrient, more potent in some ways than vitamin A. Studies suggest it helps fight cancers of the bladder, breast and cervix, and strengthens the immune system of people infected with the HIV virus. All yellow and red fruits and vegetables, and green leafy vegetables are good sources of this valuable nutrient.

I can eat mango any time. When you are feeling low, try slicing a green mango and sprinkling it with salt, sugar and a little bit of chilli. Wow!

For a real treat, roll a ripe mango in your hands until it is very soft and you can feel the stone move, cut a hole in the top and very slowly enjoy the fruit juice that you can press out. It's a joy.

Try this easy dessert. Peel and slice a ripe mango. Place the slices in a sauté pan containing a little melted butter. Warm the slices on one side, then turn and warm the other. The flesh should just begin to brown at the edges. Remove the fruit to dessert plates and sprinkle with ground ginger and salt. This can be served during the main meal. A definite success.

STUFFED DATES

Buy the best quality dates you can find. They should be plump, and the skin should be tight. Use the recipe for Toasted Nuts on page 176, but leave them unsalted for this recipe. Brazil nuts are the best sort of nut to use as they are a rich source of selenium.

Ingredients

455g/1lb/3$\frac{1}{4}$ cups dried dates.

2 cups toasted nuts

115g/4oz/1$\frac{1}{3}$ cups desiccated (shredded) coconut

1   Split each date lengthways and remove the pit. (It is worth doing this yourself, rather than buying pitted dates, because you can form the pocket into which you will place the nut as you remove the seed.)

2   Select large pieces of nut to fit into the hollow in each date. Gently open the hollow in each date and squeeze in a nut, making sure that when the date is pressed closed again, the nut will not be visible.

3   Spread a piece of greaseproof (waxed) paper in the bottom of a shallow baking pan and sprinkle liberally with the desiccated (shredded) coconut.

4   Place the dates in a microwave-proof dish, cover with microwave film, and microwave for 30 second (650 watts). This will release some moisture from the dates

5   Taking care to respect the heat that has been generated by microwaving, immediately roll each date firmly in the coconut to create a coating. (The success of this will depend on the dates, but it is worth the effort because the coconut adds to the flavour and appearance of the final product.

Dates are rich in potassium, and a good source of vitamin C. They work as a gentle laxative.

Age-defying substances in apricots include folate, which is good for the heart, and two important antioxidants: beta-carotene and vitamin C. Apricots are a good source of potassium, iron and fibre.

Ginger is a natural decongestant. A good choice when you suffer from sinus problems. Ginger in food relieves travel sickness, nausea and morning sickness, and settles the digestive system. Because it aids circulation, ginger stimulates the blood supply to the skin, keeping it young looking.

Melons contain two antioxidants that slow the onset of signs of age: vitamin C and beta-carotene. Orange-fleshed varieties contain the highest concentrations of beta-carotene. Melons are 90 per cent water, and help to flush out your system.

APRICOT CREAM

Serves 4

Ingredients

565g/1$\frac{1}{4}$lbs/2$\frac{1}{2}$ cups apricot purée

1 package/300g/10$\frac{1}{2}$oz soft, plain tofu, well drained

1 tbsp honey

1　To make the purée, place 500g/1lb/2$\frac{1}{4}$ cups dried apricots in a deep pan, cover with water, and simmer until the fruit is very soft. Cook down the water, but do not burn. Cool, and either push through a sieve, or purée in a blender. Any extra that is not used for the recipe can be stored in the refrigerator and enjoyed later with a dollop of yogurt.

2　In the same blender, place the required amount of apricot purée, the tofu and honey. Blend until smooth.

3　Pour into dessert bowls, and chill for at least 2 hours before serving.

MELON AND GINGER

Ripe Galia and Cantaloupe melons are both excellent prepared this way. Galia are best when they have changed from green to brown. This dish is excellent served with a dollop of calcium-rich Greek-style yogurt.

Serves 4

Ingredients

1 medium melon

7–8 pieces stem ginger in syrup

2–3 tbsp syrup from the ginger

1   Halve the melon and remove the seeds. Remove the flesh with a scoop or melon baller, and place in an attractive glass bowl. I like the way this looks in crystal.

2   Slice the ginger into thin pieces and sprinkle over the melon. Turn the mixture over gently with a wooden spoon.

3   Drizzle the ginger syrup over the melon. Cover the bowl and chill in the refrigerator for at least 3 hours before serving.

Scientific research tells us: soya is a source of powerful hormone-like substances that fight the signs of age; soya helps lower blood cholesterol and lipid levels, thus fighting heart disease; soya helps protect against colon cancer; the hormone-like effects of substances in soya help prevent osteoporosis and the hot sweats of menopause; certain proteins in soya boost the immune system and help fight disease; compounds in soya are thought to slow or prevent certain forms of kidney damage; studies have linked high consumption of soya with lower levels of lung cancer; studies in Japan suggest that soya in the diet lowers the risk of prostate cancer. (A good love life is a sure way to stay young, so protect your man.)

Mangoes are rich in beta-carotene, vitamin C and fruit sugars: all nutrients that slow down the onset of signs of age.

Egg yolk is an excellent source of vitamin B12, important for good memory and a healthy nervous system.

The combination of ingredients in this easy-to-digest food makes it an excellent choice when you are feeling low, or recovering from illness.

COCONUT CUSTARD WITH FRESH MANGO

Serves 4

Ingredients

1 can/425g/14 oz coconut milk, including cream

3 tbsp caster (superfine) sugar

2 tsp cornflour (cornstarch)

pinch of salt

4 egg yolks

$1/4$ tsp vanilla extract

1 tbsp dark brown sugar

2 large, ripe mangoes, peeled and sliced

1   Pour the coconut milk into a pan over medium heat and bring to the boil. Reduce the heat and cook over a low flame for 3 to 4 minutes. Remove from the heat and set aside.

2   Combine the white sugar, cornflour (cormstarch), and salt in a large mixing bowl. Add the egg yolks and whisk to combine. Slowly add 2 or 3 tablespoons of the hot coconut milk while stirring the mixture.

3   Whisk the egg and sugar mixture into the hot coconut milk in the pan and replace over medium heat. Whisk constantly until the custard is very thick; this will take 5 or 6 minutes. Add the vanilla and whisk in just before removing the pan from the heat.

4   Pour the hot custard into a serving bowl, sprinkle with the brown sugar, and allow to cool to room temperature. Arrange the mango slices on the custard, cover with cling film (plastic wrap), and refrigerate for at least an hour before serving.

Quick Reference Chart for Herbs and Food Supplements

HERBS

Herb	Use
St John's Wort	Otherwise known as Hypericum. This is the biggest selling antidepressant in Germany, out-selling Prozac. Tests have shown it to be just as effective with fewer side-effects. It can help to boost low mood and treat mild depression. It is particularly good at restoring lost interest in sex.
Black Cohosh	The dried root of the black cohosh plant contains oestrogen-like plant hormones. This herb can help to overcome some of the menopause symptoms that are due to a lowering of oestrogen levels.
Blackcurrant Leaves	Blackcurrant leaves are an effective treatment for hot sweats.
Horsetail	Horsetail is a useful herbal remedy if you are prone to night sweats.

Dandelion	The humble dandelion is a powerful diuretic and can be used to help reduce fluid retention.
Witch Hazel	This favourite childhood remedy is useful if you find that you suffer from broken capillaries in later life.
Sarsaparilla	Sarsaparilla helps to overcome a reduced sex drive in women going through menopause. However, if you have a tendency towards excess facial hair you should avoid it, as it can encourage hair growth.

HOMOEOPATHIC REMEDIES

Remedy	Use
Pulsatilla 30C	Combats low mood accompanied by an irresistible urge to cry.
Nux Vomica 30C	Useful if your low mood is connected to stress, irritability and overwork.
Calc Carb 30C	Use this homoeopathic remedy if you are suffering from anxiety with panic attacks.
Phosphorus 30C	Phosphorus 30C is recommended for continual underlying anxiety.
Glonoin 30C	Recommended for the treatment of hot sweats.
Sepia 6C	Can help to combat night sweats.
Apis 30C	Apis 30C is excellent for combating fluid retention that is accompanied by restlessness and burning hot sweats.
Bryonia 6C	A useful remedy for fluid retention accompanied by painful breasts and vaginal soreness with decreased sensitivity.
Lycopodium 30C	Another useful remedy for vaginal dryness and hot sweats.

Rekevic	This remedy will give lacklustre hair a boost.
Sepia 30C	Use Sepia 30C to treat loss of interest in sex that is severe and linked with exhaustion.
Agnus Castus 30C	Used to treat reduced sex drive that is accompanied by generally reduced energy levels.

FOOD SUPPLEMENTS

Supplement	Use
Evening Primrose Oil	This is a rich source of Essential Fatty Acids. It can be useful in the treatment of breast pain, menopausal symptoms, dry skin and lacklustre hair. It is most effective when combined with supplements of vitamin E.
Spirulina	Spirulina is a fresh-water algae, which has the richest iron content known in nature. It also contains more vitamin E than wheatgerm, and more vitamin B12 than raw beef. It is especially useful if you suffer from cellulite or wish to improve the condition of your hair.

Further Reading

Beauty Wisdom: The Secret of Looking Good and Feeling Fabulous,
  Bharti Vyas with Claire Haggard, Thorsons
The Anti-Cellulite Plan, Liz Hodgkinson, Thorsons
What Your Doctor May Not Tell You About the Menopause, John R Lee
  MD, Warner Books
The Menopause, Dr Jean Coope, Dunitz
Miracle Sleep Cure, James B Maas, Thorsons
Menopause without Weight Gain, Debra Waterhouse, Thorsons
  (*Outsmarting the Mid-Life Fat Cell*, Hyperion)
The Menopause, Dr Sarah Brewer, Thorsons
Making Love Better Than Ever, Barbara Keesling Ph.D., Hunter House
Healing Mind, Healthy Woman, Alice D. Domar and Henry Dreher,
  Thorsons
Self Esteem, Gael Lindenfield, Thorsons
The Positive Woman, Gael Lindenfield, Thorsons
The Plants We Need to Eat, Jeannette Ewin, Thorsons
Aromatherapy for Women, Maggie Tisserand, Thorsons
The Fats We Need To Eat, Jeannette Ewin, Thorsons
Super Skin, Kathryn Marsden, Thorsons
Skin Problems, Thorsons Natural Health
The Hormone Dilemma, Dr Susan M Love with Karen Lindsey, Thorsons
Anti-Wrinkle Plan, Anita Guyton, Thorsons

Stop Ageing Now!, Jean Carper, Thorsons

Ageless Beauty The Natural Way, Anita Guyton, Thorsons

Skin Tricks, Dr Gerald Imber, Thorsons

Menopause Without Medicine, Linda Ojeda, Thorsons

Natural Healing for Women, Susan Curtis and Romy Fraser, Thorsons

Acupressure for Health, Jacqueline Young, Thorsons

Acupressure Made Easy, Dr Julian Kenyon, Thorsons

Plate section: Picture Credits

Index

Simply

Radiant